Jesus the Rabbi

Dwain Miller

JESUS THE RABBI

ISBN: 918-1-939779-04-5

Published by

LIFEBRIDGE
BOOKS
P.O. Box 49428
Charlotte, NC 28277

Cover illustration by Art Slatten.
Printed in the United States of America.

Dedication

This book is dedicated to my wonderful wife, Debbie, for her love and support during the many blessed years of our marriage.

Contents

FOREWORD
BY PERRY STONE

When ministers study each week to find a Word from the Lord for their congregation, most with academic backgrounds research detailed information from numerous commentaries of former scholars and Bible teachers. Much of the research is presented from the Greek-Roman way of thinking. However, one of the greatest methods of biblical study is to dig deep into the well of Hebraic thought—as the New Testament was written by predominantly Jewish men who understood the Torah, the Law, and the prophets.

Often ministers camp out in the New Testament, studying the Greek language to enhance their subject matter, and unwittingly ignore the Old Testament language of Hebrew with the customs and oral traditions of the Jewish people that helped form the thinking of the New Testament church.

In this unique book, Pastor Dwain Miller has tapped into an amazing and lesser known Hebraic method of how Christ went through a special process to become a Master Rabbi. I will not outline any information in this foreword, but I will tell you that you are about to learn one of the most amazing narratives in the life of Christ that will open the eyes of your understanding to the "yoke of Christ" that believers are to put on. This "yoke" is not what you may think it is.

You will enjoy this book and will want to read it several times to glean from the powerful and fresh truth contained on its pages. As you are about to learn, Pastor Dwain is a skilled communicator and writer. Enjoy discovering the "Jewish Jesus" and taking on His "yoke"!

– Perry Stone, Jr., Founder and Director,
Voice of Evangelism Ministries Cleveland, TN

Introduction

Do you ask questions when you read biblical accounts of the life of Jesus? I know I do! Do you sometimes wish the Holy Spirit had given us more revelation that filled in the blanks of Jesus' life, especially during those years from His birth to thirty years of age, when He began His public ministry?

This book, *Jesus The Rabbi*, contains many of the answers to these questions. Such as:

- Where was Jesus from age twelve, when we see Him in the temple being interviewed by the Pharisees, until age thirty when He arrives to be baptized by John the Baptist?
- What exactly did His baptism mean? And, why was the Son of God baptized in the first place?
- Why did they call Him Rabbi? Was this simply a common slang title handed out to anyone who attempted to teach the Torah?
- By what authority did Jesus just stroll up into a synagogue, pick up a scroll of Isaiah and begin teaching? Wasn't that a very sacred ministry reserved for a select few?
- Why did He command such a great following of listeners? Did the people of His day have nothing better to do than abandon their personal responsibilities and just hang out with a "rebel" religious guy all day long?

I think you get my point!

Jesus The Rabbi is designed to "fill in the blanks" for you in many areas of the life and ministry of Jesus. I truly believe that we have attempted to explain Him through a *western culture* mindset. However, life and work of Jesus is impossible to interpret outside of the Hebrew culture. The fact is, Jesus is a Jew. Not only a Jew, but during His time on the earth, He was a trained and qualified Rabbi—who had verified authority to be the leading teacher of His day. This authority was termed *schemica*. This was the calling card that attracted thousands to follow after Him and His teaching. It was the draw that caused grown men to abandon all responsibilities to become His disciples.

If you are a serious student of the Scripture and follower of Christ, this book will establish in you a cultural context that will enable you to clearly interpret the teachings of God's Son.

Join me for a fascinating journey into the life of *Jesus The Rabbi!*

– Dwain Miller

CHAPTER 1

DO YOU SEE WHAT I HEAR?

We live in a culture that has, for centuries now, cultivated the idea that the skeptical person is always smarter than one who believes. You can almost be as stupid as a cabbage as long as you doubt.

– DALLAS WILLARD

In his inspiring sermon "How to Hear God Speak," Rick Warren talks about the problem of distractions that keep us from listening to the Lord: "Many of you did what I did last Mother's Day. You picked up the phone and dialed your mom to say, 'Happy Mother's Day.' And as you were doing it, you got the same little message, 'Sorry, but all the circuits are busy.' Everybody else in America was calling their mothers.

"Many times, God has wanted to talk to you, but He got a busy signal. Many times God has wanted to talk to you in your life, but the line was off the hook and you don't want to do call waiting with God. You've got to make time. When you're too busy—and there are many things that are good but can distract you—you're too busy to listen to God."

I must admit, there have been occasions in my own life and ministry I was too busy to hear my heavenly Father's voice. It's not that I didn't want to hear Him; other priorities filled my day. I have been in ministry for over twenty-seven years. I have spent at least nine years in studying and receiving special degrees. Some would even say I've been educated beyond my intelligence. While that may be true, the facts are the facts. As the old ball player Dizzy Dean used to say, "It ain't bragging if you've done it!" I must admit there have been times when God wanted to speak to me but I was too busy doing "ministry" to hear His voice.

There came a point when I realized I didn't know everything about God. I knew I didn't want to serve a God I couldn't get my head around. Instead of allowing my pride to put up a roadblock, I determined to open my heart and let the Lord say anything He wanted. The first step to receiving revelation is admitting you don't know it all, and I sure didn't!

Lately, there are days when I feel like Elijah on top of Mount Carmel. Not that I consider myself a prophet, or have ever had to confront 450 false prophets or call down fire from heaven. No, but we do have one thing in common. After wiping out all of the false prophets, during a great drought, Elijah told King Ahab, "You need to leave now, I hear the sound of abundance of rain."

No one else heard it but him. The king didn't hear it. The onlookers didn't hear it. Not even Elijah's personal assistant heard it. Seven times he told his servant to go and watch for rain. Six times he came back and said there is nothing. On the seventh try he returned and told him, "I see a cloud the size of a man's hand."

Instead of feeling disappointed with such a small answer to his big faith, Elijah said, "It's time to go, the storm is coming!" You know the rest of the story. He heard it before he saw it. Like Elijah, I have been hearing before seeing. Once I slowed down long enough to hear God speak, my life has been forever imprinted by His voice.

Needed Revelation

There is one thing that constantly amazes me. For centuries the church has been given volumes of knowledge, and yet with all of this information, so little change has taken place. Of course there have been exceptions, but for the most part, change has come slowly. If information and knowledge could win the world for Christ we would have accomplished the mission a long time ago. We don't need more information, what we need is "revelation." After all, how many life-changing sermons can you hear in one year?

If you are a faithful and loyal church member and only miss on average four Sunday's a year that leaves forty eight Sundays to hear life-changing messages. If you attend both services, you now have ninety-six such sermons, I mean really, how many do you need? If we taught our kids in school the way we teach people in church we would teach the ABC's on Monday and by Friday have them write a book report on War and Peace! We keep piling on new teaching week after week and never let people digest and work through what they've already heard!

For several years now I have been "hearing" revelation that is constantly impacting my life. A major theme the Holy Spirit has been showing me is that there is a difference between listening and hearing. Listening will get you information and knowledge; hearing revelation will change you from the inside out.

Wouldn't it be great if God decided to use road signs along the highway to talk to us? Just think, we could drive down the road and the Lord would simply choose one of a hundred signs to grab our attention. Or, better yet, an angel would paint the top of barns with a message straight from heaven. Let's face it, "See Rock City" is getting a little boring. We'd be cruising along with a mapped out message straight from God. Now that's what I would call awesome. Only one problem: it doesn't work that way.

I've often thought this method would certainly work for me! On the other hand, God could use something more subtle. Like a gentle rap on the side of the head whenever we veer off course. There's a thought! God smacking people whenever they don't listen. I'm afraid we'd all be walking around in a daze from all that rapping "activity."

Of course, you could be one of the fortunate ones like Moses, who was walking up the side of a mountain, minding his own business, when he stumbled upon the burning bush. Most of us don't have those kinds of encounters so we find ourselves looking for skills to help us hear from God.

We are all products of those who taught us. When salvation was presented to us, you and I had someone imprint their spiritual DNA into our system. I once heard a preacher say this about new converts in his church, "Oh God, please don't let them catch on and think that it's somehow normal to be a dead, nominal Sunday morning saint."

WHO IMPRINTED YOU?

Sandy Warner, in his book, *Eagle Facts and Parables of Mentoring,* shares these facts:

> *Did you know that eagles must learn to fly and hunt by observing their parents? These skills are not instinctive like some of God's creatures. However, eagles are born with a different instinct called imprinting. Konrad Lorenz first discovered imprinting when he observed ducks and geese hatching out of their eggs. He noticed they would bond with the first moving object they saw, regardless of whether this was their parent. From that first moment of imprinting, they follow their moving parent (or adopted parent) until raised.*
>
> *Lorenz demonstrated how incubator-hatched geese would imprint on the first suitable moving stimulus they saw within what he called a 'critical period' between 13–16 hours shortly after hatching. For example, the goslings would imprint on Lorenz himself (to be more specific, on his wading boots), and he is often depicted being followed by a gaggle of geese who had imprinted on him. Lorenz also found that the geese could imprint on inanimate objects.*
>
> *In one experiment, they followed a box placed on a model train in circles around the track. Filial imprinting is not restricted to non-human animals that are able to follow their parents, however. In child development, the term is used to refer to the process by which a baby learns who its mother and father are. The process is recognized as beginning in the womb, when the unborn baby starts to recognize its parents' voices. (It is interesting that Paul said, "Imitate me, just as I also imitate Christ"* (1 Corinthians 11:1).

Can you imagine the horror a young eaglet would feel if it was imprinted by a chicken? The young eagle knows there is something different about him, he just can't seem to jive with the rest of the barnyard. While the other chickens keep their head down all day looking for something to peck, the young eagle is looking skyward yearning to soar. He notices when a storm comes the chicks run for cover while he has the urge to climb high on the thermals. Everything inside him screams, "I don't belong here, I don't speak chicken—I speak eagle!"

Now, imagine a new Christian who is imprinted by a person who does not believe the Bible is the inspired, infallible Word of God. Someone who does not believe miracles are for today or the Holy Spirit still gives gifts to His children. Sitting in a pew (the barnyard) knowing there has to be more to the Christian life than just attending church on Sunday. Every time the young Christian is told that you can't expect healing, or have authority over the devil, he looks skyward yearning to soar. One day, somewhere, at some point you're going to see someone stand up on Sunday morning and scream, "I don't speak chicken—I speak eagle!"

The most difficult men and women to reach with revelation aren't the new Christians. No, it's the ones who were imprinted years ago. Their motto is, "Don't bother me with facts, my mind is made up." The religious crowd has all the answers. If what you're doing can be explained, more than likely God is not in it.

A nation or civilization that continues to produce soft-minded men purchases its own spiritual death on the installment plan.

– MARTIN LUTHER KING, JR.

The best thing that can happen to a new convert is to be given a Bible, lock them away from the religious crowd, and let them study God's Word for at least two years. I promise you they will come out of that experience believing in the power of God, miracles, signs and wonders, and all the other promises the Lord made to His church.

The 19th-century Danish theologian, Soren Kierkegaard,

identified two kinds of religion: Religion A and Religion B. The first is "faith" in name only (2 Timothy 3:5). It's the practice of attending church without genuine faith in the living Lord.

Religion B, on the other hand, is a life-transforming, destiny-changing experience. It's a definite commitment to the crucified and risen Savior, which establishes an ongoing personal relationship between a forgiven sinner and a gracious God.

This difference explains why for many years British author C. S. Lewis had such great difficulty in becoming a Christian. Religion A had blinded him to Religion B. According to his brother Warren, his conversion was "no sudden plunge into a new life, but rather a slow, steady convalescence from a deep-seated spiritual illness—an illness that had its origins in our childhood, in the dry husks of religion offered by the semi-political churchgoing of Ulster, and the similar dull emptiness of compulsory church during our school days."

TIPPING OVER RELIGIOUS COWS

There has been much debate over the idea that you can tip over a cow. Most researchers agree it's nothing more than an urban legend. The premise is to sneak up on an unsuspecting cow, while she is asleep, and tip her over.

First, cows don't sleep standing up, and second, I'm told that trying to push over a cow is like trying to push over a bus. Third, why would you want to do it anyway? After my research I have come to the conclusion it really doesn't matter whether it's fact or fiction. If someone wants to waste their time trying to push over an unsuspecting cow, good luck to them!

However, there are certain religious cows that need tipping over. Some are just as hard to tip as trying to sneak up on a cow! History is littered with the bones of much greater men than I who have tried it. Still, I'm going to make an attempt.

Let's examine three of the most popular.

1. We have never done it that way before.

Many times we do things without knowing why, but we do it

anyway. Because we have always done it in a certain manner and no one has taken the time to find out why for themselves, we go through life doing those same things. After so many years of this repetition, the concrete wall of tradition is built up.

The story is told about a wife preparing a roast. She carefully cuts off the end of the roast, puts the roast in a pan and then in the oven. The husband asks her, "Why did you cut the end off?" She replies, "Because my mom always did."

The next day the wife talks to her mom and asks, "Why did you cut the end off of the roast before putting it in the oven?" Mom replies, "Because my mom always did." So both of them went to grandma and asked the same question. "Grandma, why do you cut the end of the roast off before cooking it?" Grandma replies, "So it would fit in to the pan!"

Traditions are powerful enemies of change because they are full of security. It's a fact that when we do those things that we've always done, we don't have to think about it.

We lose the incentive to grow. Creative ideas, and new ways will interfere with the conventional way of "what we have always done."

We allow man's customs to take precedent over God's Word.

Let's be clear, I do not believe that all traditions are wrong. We don't need to throw out the baby with the bathwater! Some important traditions have been passed down from generation to generation. The danger lies in making them equal to the commandments of God. When we do, we transition from traditions to traditionalism.

A tradition is a custom or habit that becomes part of the expected church culture. Traditionalism, however, is valuing traditions as unwritten laws which are over, above, and therefore against the Word of God.

Tradition is the living faith of those now dead.
Traditionalism is the dead faith of those still living.

– JAROSLAV PELIKAN

On more than one occasion we have substituted our personal

taste (whether it be a certain style of music, or a preferred version of the Bible) over the clear teachings of Scripture. Just because someone doesn't like the same music that I prefer doesn't make me right and them wrong. If it's a matter of taste and preference, show grace. If it's a matter of the clear teaching of the Word of God, stand firm. I suppose that's why Baskin-Robbins makes 31 flavors of ice cream, not everyone's taste buds are the same!

Traditions that once served their purpose well when started, could actually negate the creation of new things that might be better. One of the biggest enemies of each generation is what was "working well" in the last generation. Sadly, the modern church always seems to lag behind the learning curve. Instead of allowing God to infuse us with new and creative ideas, by and large we turn to the world system to show us what to do.

Under the category of some of the dumbest things I've ever heard is a popular pastor who said, "I will never use a Bible program on my computer. It will become too easy, and God expects me to work hard when I study." Of course, I heard later that he changed his mind when he discovered that he could do twice the amount of study in half the amount of time.

When we fall into the trap of the common attitude, "We have never done it that way before," we build a prison by which we shut down the voice of God in exchange for the "comfort of the known." The Lord is under no obligation to move on our behalf if we refuse to change. He will always find someone else to do what we are unwilling to do.

It's been said, "If you want something you never had, you must be willing to try things you've never done!"

Even Jesus, the greatest leader/teacher who ever lived, was accused of breaking sacred traditions (See Matthew 15:1-15). I could give you several examples, but let's look at one in particular:

The disciples of Jesus were caught red-handed, not washing their hands before a meal. *"Why do your disciples break the tradition of the elders? They don't wash their hands before they eat!"* (Matthew 15:2 NIV).

I think we would all agree it is a good thing to wash our hands. Jesus was not saying that it was a bad idea. The real issue was that the elders considered washing your hands before you eat was God's law (See Exodus 30:17-21), not a matter of proper hygiene. However, you cannot find anywhere that God made a law which says we are to wash our hands before eating. Quite the contrary, it was for Aaron and his sons to wash before they performed duties in the tabernacle. The Pharisees did what they always did. They extended the rule from the priest to all people.

Jesus did not flinch. He made it very clear by challenging their tradition. *"And why do you break the command of God for the sake of your tradition?"* (Matthew 15:3 NIV).

Jesus addressed the very heart of the difference between man-made rules and God's law. He was constantly confronted by the religious leaders of His day and yet He did not back away from the challenge. He refused to allow them to place burdens of traditionalism on His followers. In Matthew 23:4 (NIV), He said, *"They tie up heavy loads and put them on men's shoulders, but they themselves are not willing to lift a finger to move them."*

This leads us to the second cow that needs tipping over.

2. What we think we know.

I think it's time for a little confession. Someone said, "Confession is good for the soul but bad for the reputation." I'm willing to take the risk. I confess I don't have all the answers. There I said it, and guess what, you don't either! The first step in hearing revelation is admitting you have more to learn.

Simon Peter thought he had it all figured out (See Acts 10).

His whole life he was taught not to eat what was unclean. That was the law, it was in the book, no exceptions. Like so many of us, Peter had built a theological house of cards. Little did he know that when the wind of the Holy Spirit blew through the upper room in Acts 2, not only was he filled and baptized with the Spirit, his house of cards would crash and burn. What he thought he knew was about to radically change, as we read in Acts 10. Have you noticed as soon as you think you have God figured out, He does something to blow up all you thought you knew? Peter would admit, "I can certainly testify to that!"

At one point, Peter was staying with Simon, a tanner (forbidden by law). On the rooftop, heaven opened and the Lord showed him a vision of all sorts of unclean animals. God told him to "rise and eat." Peter protested because he knew the law said differently. Peter would not be the first nor the last to argue his theological position with God, as if the Almighty needed instruction!

The Lord took a sledgehammer and knocked down another wall of his tradition. *"What God has cleansed you must not call common"* (Acts 10:15). So, while Peter was munching on a bag of pork rinds, he explained to the rest of the leadership what God was doing with the Gentiles. As the debate raged, all Peter could say was, "Guys, I had a dream, God is changing all the rules, that's all I know."

The disciples of Jesus thought they had it all figured out (See John 9).

The disciples believed that a man was born blind because of his sin or because of the sin of his parents. They asked Jesus, *"Rabbi, who sinned, this man or his parents, that he was born blind?"* (John 9:2).

Don't be too hard on them. They were only repeating what they had been taught. When we see something we've never seen before, our default position is to always refer back to "what we think we know." Most arguments and debates in the church concerning revelation always start with the default position. Therefore, we close our minds to the understanding that God may be doing a work we've never seen before.

The Pharisees thought they had it all figured out.

Some of the Pharisees argued, *"This man is not from God, for he does not keep the Sabbath"* (verse 16). Not only did they consider the blind man to be a lawbreaker, but refused to believe that Jesus was the Messiah. The Pharisees even forced this poor man's own parents into the charade by threatening to put them out of the synagogue if they acknowledged a miracle had taken place.

All of them were holding to the same traditions. They believed blindness was caused by breaking God's law and anyone who broke the Sabbath law could not be of God, therefore sin was the root cause.

Notice how each reacted to the same event:

- The disciples were willing to learn, and change their assumption in response to Jesus' words and deeds.
- The blind man was willing to change based on his personal experience. He was blind—now he could see! His experience trumped the law.
- The Pharisees, saw the same event, but refused to change their assumptions and, as a result, became morally and spiritually blind.

I thought I had it all figured out.

Jesus only resisted those who thought they knew it all. I did not want to be included in that group. I did not want to be so proud of my theological education and ministry experience to brag that I had it all together. Of course, there are some things I believe that form the core values of my life.

These truths are the solid foundation I stand on:

- I believe in the virgin birth of Jesus.
- I believe in the blood atonement for my sins.
- I believe the Bible is the inspired, infallible Word of God.
- I believe in the death, burial, and resurrection of Jesus.
- I believe in the second coming of the Savior.
- I believe miracles, and gifts of the Spirit are for the church today.

There is something else I believe; I have so much more to learn. You see, the final test of truth and ministry is determined by the spirit in which it's given. If I stand up and tell you what I am preaching is a fact from the word of God, I had better be able to back it up. I could develop a hard spirit that communicates, "Don't confuse me with the Bible, my mind is made up." I can even be right, but if my spirit is wrong, the message is wrong. Conversely, if my spirit is right I may be wrong about some things, but I am willing to open my spiritual understanding for greater truth. Peter said we are to be established in *"present truth."* (2 Peter 1:12).

Jesus wants us to speak the truth in love and demonstrate grace. If you want to see an illustration of this, all you have to do is look at the ministry of a couple named Aquila and Priscilla. In Acts 18:24-26, we read the account of a young preacher named Apollos. After listening to this man who was *"instructed in the way of the Lord; and being fervent in the spirit, he spoke and taught accurately the things of the Lord, though he only knew the baptism of John."*

Aquila and Priscilla did not run out of the building to announce that the preacher was not telling the whole story. They didn't get mad and move their membership. No, they took him aside and explained a more excellent way, with kindness and love. What was the result? *"He greatly helped those who had believed through grace, for he vigorously refuted the Jews publicly, showing from the Scriptures that Jesus is the Christ"* (verses 27-28).

Finally, there is one more sacred cow that needs tipping over.

3. Not here, not now, and not that way!

In Luke 13:10-17, we are told that Jesus was teaching in one of the synagogues on the Sabbath. There was a woman who was bound by a spirit of infirmity for eighteen years. Since love rules over the law, Jesus called her and said, *"Woman, you are loosed from your infirmity. He laid His hands on her, and immediately she was made straight, and glorified God."*

I would think the expected result would be the ruler of the synagogue jumped for joy and shouted, "Hallelujah!" After all, I'm sure he knew the woman personally and by name. No doubt he had seen her at the synagogue for years. I can imagine each Sabbath she would come in struggling, all bent over. The ruler of the synagogue would stoop down to greet her. If this were in the modern church, her name would be on the prayer chain every week. The phone lines would be buzzing with, "Please pray for our dear sister, you know how much she suffers. I just wish there was something we could do."

However, that wasn't the response in Jerusalem. *"But the ruler of the synagogue answered with indignation because Jesus had healed on the Sabbath; and he said to the crowd, 'there are six days on which men ought to work; therefore, and be healed on them and not on the Sabbath day'"* (Luke 13:14). In essence He was complaining, "Not here, not now, and not that way!"

Sadly, in the average church, it's all right to talk about healing just as long as no one gets healed. It's even okay to talk about anointing with oil for healing just as long as you don't do it. We blindly believe that talking about something changes the circumstances. As hard as it is to believe, churches have split apart over the issue of healing, styles of worship, and spiritual gifts.

Jesus would have none of it. The Lord then answered the ruler of the synagogue, saying, *"Hypocrite! Does not each one of you on the Sabbath loose his ox or donkey from the stall, and lead it away to water it? So ought not this woman, being a daughter of Abraham, whom Satan has bound—think of it—for eighteen years, be loosed from this bond on the Sabbath?"* (verses 13:15-17).

Jesus used one of the strongest words to describe the ruler's attitude; *hypocrite*. The word really means "an actor," one who wears a mask or one who pretends. The principal criticism of Jesus toward the Pharisees is they taught one thing, yet did another.

In his book, *The Four Loves*, C. S. Lewis warns, "Anyone who has ever taught or attempted to lead others knows the tendency in all of us toward exaggerating our depth of character while treating leniently our flaws. The Bible calls this tendency hypocrisy. We consciously or subconsciously put forward a better image of ourselves than really exists. The outward appearance of our character and the inner reality (that only God, we, and perhaps our family members know) do not match."

We must all heed the warning of Jesus. Just because we have never seen it does not necessarily mean it's not of God. Many times our arrogance and pride will block new revelation from heaven. More than once it has been said, "I don't believe in miracles." My reply would be, "You may not believe in miracles until you need one!" God has some unique ways of changing our heart.

Throw a person who believes God's miracles are only for yesterday in a lion's den and watch their theology change.
– TOMMY TENNEY

There was another ruler of the synagogue, but this man had a dramatic change of heart. His name was Jairus. It is amazing what a crisis will do to your theological viewpoint. I can't say for sure if he had the same attitude as the one we read about in Luke 13, but this one thing I know, when his daughter was dying, he didn't care about tradition or the law. He sent for Jesus and begged Him to come and lay hands on her *"that she may be healed, and she will live"* (Mark 5:23).

When desperation rises above the level of arrogance and pride you will seek out a person who believes in miracles!

The age-old argument is, "God is not writing any more Bible." I agree, He's not. The inference is, of course, "I already know everything God has said or written, therefore there's nothing new under the sun."

There are some who believe when the Canon of Scripture was complete, God put tape over His mouth and stopped talking. There is only one thing wrong with that position— it's not true!

There was a young preacher in his first year of ministry who stood up and declared to his congregation, "I'm going to take a year and preach through the entire Bible." It was reported after many decades of ministry he confessed, "After all these years I haven't even scratched the surface."

I believe God is releasing to each generation more revelation about what He has already written in His Word. We don't need more Bible, we need more spiritual understanding of what has already been written. Like a time-release cold pill, I believe each new generation receives another spiritual dose of anointed revelation. The tragedy is this: many are so imprinted by their upbringing, denominational biases, or just plain stubbornness, that when new revelation is released they are not able to receive, because it doesn't fit their theological box.

People of grace and love can disagree on certain aspects of revelation and still love each other. One thing we can all agree on is that God is in charge, and we are not! As far as I know He has never asked my opinion about what He should do. I don't get a vote! It's His house, therefore He can rearrange the furniture anytime He pleases!

IT'S TIME TO PUT ON YOUR SPIRITUAL EARS

Back in the 70s when everyone had CB radios, the most popular phrase was, "Hey, good buddy, do you have your ears on?" God is still speaking today and He wants to know if we have our spiritual ears on? *"Whoever has ears, let them hear what the Spirit says to the churches"* (Revelation 3:22).

In his wonderful devotional book, *My Utmost For His Highest*, Oswald Chambers writes, "Get into the habit of saying, 'Speak, Lord,' and life will become a romance. Every time circumstances press in on you say, 'Speak, Lord,' and make time to listen. Chastening is more than a means of discipline—it is meant to bring me to the point of saying, 'Speak, Lord.' Think back to a time when God spoke to you. Do you remember what He said? As we listen, our ears become more sensitive, and like Jesus, we will hear God all the time."

FIVE HINDRANCES TO HEARING GOD'S VOICE

1. ***The true sheep will hear the voice of the Shepherd and will be led by Him*** (John 10:1-5).

God speaks to you every day; however, if your receiver is clogged, you won't hear His instructions. Make sure you are a sheep and not a goat.

2. ***Unbelief hinders your ability to hear from God.***

Unbelief will cause me to distrust the Lord, which leads to

doubt and confusion (Romans 4:20). If you don't believe what God says, then His Word won't work for you. We must learn to trust our heavenly Father, even if we can't see the fulfillment of His promises right away.

3. An undeveloped spirit-man hinders your ability to hear from God.

Some are more developed in their emotions than they are in their spirit-man, therefore emotions rule the day. God's desire is that we be whole so that we can hear His voice clearly (1 Thessalonians 5:23-24). God's Word is the connection to manifestation; therefore, you must fill your spirit with Scripture.

4. A spirit of deafness hinders your ability to hear from God.

This is not a physical problem but a spiritual one (Hebrews 5:11-14). Unforgiveness, focusing on painful memories, anger, jealousy, bitterness, and resentment grieves the Holy Spirit and causes deafness to overtake you (Ephesians 4:26-31).

5. Neglect hinders your ability to hear from God.

When you neglect prayer, Bible study and fellowship with the Lord, it affects your thoughts, actions, habits, character and destiny, because you are no longer aligned with God and His Word. If you want to fulfill your destiny, you must ensure that your mindset and decisions line up with His Word.

Pastor Aaron Bartmess writes, "When I was a teenager, I worked as a busboy at a restaurant. One very busy Friday evening an older man approached me with a look of both amusement and irritation. He said to me, 'Son, I've been coming to this restaurant for 10 years, and in all that time I have NEVER seen a sign like that!' He pointed to our 'Please Wait to be Seated' sign sitting at the entrance to the restrooms!

"In all the hectic scramble, one of the other employees moved the sign because it had gotten in the way. But in his rush to get on with things, he forgot that the sign bore a message! It had become, for him, just another piece of restaurant furniture. That's what happens when you work around a sign long enough—you forget its message.

"As Christians, it's easy for us to become so familiar with God's Word that we forget that we NEED to hear its message. We forget that God intends to do more than just speak to us—He intends to change us with His Word. These lapses have us treating God's Word like a piece of furniture blending into the background, never to be examined too closely. We must take the time to look at God's Word carefully. We must pray that God, by His Spirit, would show us how relevant it is to our lives" (James 1:25).

I'm convinced that flying is something people do after they have exhausted all other means of transportation. If you are flying, you know one of the last things before takeoff is the flight attendant gives instructions. Many times it's tempting to let your mind wander and not pay attention. One instruction they always give is; "If the cabin should lose pressure, the oxygen mask will drop down; place it over your face and breathe normally."

Think about that statement for a minute? You're flying along at 35,000 feet and all of a sudden the oxygen mask drops in front of your face. I'm not sure, but breathing normally may not be the thing most people would automatically do. Scream, hyperventilate, or pray, yes. But breathing normally may not fit the category.

I have some insight to share with you in the following chapters that may not fit your God box. Put your spiritual ears on and, just in case the oxygen mask falls down, try to breathe normally if you can. If you can't, pray for revelation, that usually helps!

Now some of us may think that we know it all! But we know in part, and that is why trust is still needed no matter how much God tells us, or how clearly He speaks to us. He leads us. He doesn't push us. He doesn't hand us a map and send us on our way without Him. He wants us to keep our eyes on Him, and follow Him one step at a time. Step by step. Step by step.

– JOYCE MEYER

CHAPTER 2

TWO WORDS THAT CHANGED HISTORY

Watch your thoughts; they become words.
Watch your words; they become actions.
Watch your actions, they become habits.
Watch your habits, they become character.
Watch your character; it becomes your destiny.
– FRANK OUTLAW

Words are powerful. Within each word is a seed that can grow into monumental change. Throughout the centuries men and women have spoken words that altered the course of history. Some were uttered during times of crisis while others were spoken to inspire greatness. Either way, speech as a means of communication is the most effective tool God created for mankind.

Think of the impact made by John F. Kennedy, in his Inaugural Address as President, January 20, 1961: "And so, my fellow Americans: ask not what your country can do for you—ask what you can do for your country. My fellow citizens of the world: ask not what America will do for you, but what together we can do for the freedom of man."

With that speech, a nation was inspired to go beyond the boundaries of current thought, and land a man on the moon.

Or consider the rousing rhetoric given by Winston Churchill to the House of Commons in England on June 4, 1940: "We shall defend our Island, whatever the cost may be, we shall fight on the beaches, we shall fight on the landing grounds, we shall fight in the fields and in the streets, we shall fight in the hills; we shall never surrender."

At that moment, Great Britain was on the verge of collapse. By the power of words, a nation on the edge of extinction rose up to victory.

Look at the founding of the United States. In the Declaration of Independence, July 4, 1776, Thomas Jefferson wrote: "We hold these truths to be self-evident, that all men are created equal; that they are endowed by their Creator with inherent and inalienable Rights; that among these, are Life, Liberty, and the pursuit of Happiness."

Jefferson penned those words to forever establish the equality of man, and declared that it is the Creator who bestows our unalienable rights.

There have been others:

- Martin Luther King, Jr. spoke of a dream; and race relations changed.
- President Ronald Reagan said, "Tear down this wall"; and communism fell.
- President Abraham Lincoln proclaimed that a house divided cannot stand; and the Emancipation Proclamation was birthed.

You change your world by changing your words...
Remember, death and life are in the power of the tongue.
– JOEL OSTEEN

TWO SIMPLE WORDS THAT CHANGED THE COURSE OF HISTORY

The pages of history are filled with outstanding speeches, inspiring words, but none more powerful than two simple words that one Man spoke on the edge of the Sea of Galilee. What were they? "Follow Me." Who spoke them? Jesus of Nazareth.

As Jesus was walking beside the Sea of Galilee, he saw two brothers, Simon called Peter and his brother Andrew. They were casting a net into the lake, for they were fishermen. "Come, follow me," Jesus said, "and I will send you out to fish for people."

At once they left their nets and followed him. Going on from there, he saw two other brothers, James son of Zebedee and his brother John. They were in a boat with their father Zebedee, preparing their nets. Jesus called them, and immediately they left the boat and their father and followed him (Matthew 4:18: 22 NIV).

As he walked along, he saw Levi son of Alphaeus sitting at the tax collector's booth. "Follow me," Jesus told him, and Levi got up and followed him (Mark 2:14 NIV).

Step back in time with me to the Sea of Galilee.

It was a routine workday. Men were sitting in a boat, fishing, mending their nets, and doing what fisherman do. They were professionals. This was their job, and how they fed their families. All of a sudden a Man walks to the edge of the shore and speaks in a loud voice, "Follow Me." Without hesitation they dropped their nets, left their fishing gear and followed Him.

On another occasion, Jesus walks by a man sitting at a table collecting taxes. He was probably collecting from the men who were fishing. Jesus stops and looks at the man and says, "Follow Me."

What would cause these individuals to stop what they were doing, leave their jobs and follow a stranger? What was it about Him that would inspire these grown individuals, who were professional fisherman, to leave everything behind and walk into the unknown?

Simon Peter was one of those sitting in the boat. Just imagine the conversation he had when he returned home. He tells his wife, "Sweetheart, I'm quitting the fishing business and going to follow a man named Jesus." She looks at him and exclaims, "Why in the world would you do such a thing? You love the fishing business and you're good at it. Why would you want to give this up?" He gives an astounding reply, "I have no idea, but when He spoke, something happened on the inside of me, and I have to follow Him. I don't know the outcome or where it's going to lead.

All I know is there was something in His voice that stirred my heart. I can't explain it with words, but I know this is what I have to do."

What was it that caused such a response?

- Was it His personality?
- Was it His charisma and charm?
- Did He offer riches and wealth?
- Did He promise they would travel and become famous?
- Did He say, "Follow Me and I will show you miracles"?

It's easy for us to look back and see what transpired. We can read what it cost these men to follow Jesus. From their point of view they had no idea what the future held.

It takes more than a dynamic personality to cause grown professionals to stop what they're doing and follow without an explanation. Twelve times Jesus uttered the words, "Follow Me," and twelve men immediately responded to His call.

They didn't know:

- Their names would be forever recorded in the Bible.
- They would be preached about for over 2,000 years.
- They would be slandered as a cult following a false teacher.
- They would eventually die for answering the call to follow Christ Jesus.

The only thing they knew for sure was that their spirit was awakened when they heard His voice. They didn't know the end from the beginning—or about the fine print at the bottom of the contract!

To understand the implications of those two words, "Follow Me," we have to grasp the meaning of a familiar passage of Scripture. I believe it has been misapplied for centuries. Once we realize what Jesus meant, then we have a better understanding why these men chose to leave everything to follow Him.

A LIFE-CHANGING PASSAGE

Jesus said, *"Come to me, all you who are weary and burdened, and I will give you rest. Take my yoke upon you and learn from me, for I am gentle and humble in heart, and you will find rest for your souls. For my yoke is easy and my burden is light"* (Matthew 11:28-30 NIV).

Many wonderful sermons have been preached on these verses and lives have been touched, but there may be a cultural context we need to understand. When we consider that Jesus may have been talking about something deeper than the traditional interpretation, it will shed light on the entire ministry of Christ. He was always speaking on two levels: first, to the natural hearing, and second, to the ears of the heart.

The disciples asked again and again, "What did you mean by that teaching?" Jesus would then sit them down and explain the deeper meaning. So it is with this familiar passage of Scripture.

Let's summarize a traditional interpretation of Matthew 11:28-30. Imagine yourself as an ox, and God's Law is a huge, heavily loaded cart we are supposed to pull. All by ourselves we can't do it. As Paul says, "The good I want to do, I don't. The evil I don't want, that I keep on doing."

But now God's Son has become our brother, and placed Himself under this yoke with us—and is pulling the cart of God's Law on our behalf. Because Jesus has done this perfectly, our keeping the Law perfectly is easy. For us, it's just a matter of being yoked with Jesus, trusting in Him, then walking by His side.

This walk is no longer difficult because He is gentle and humble. He loves us and picks us up whenever we stumble.

Of course, the traditional sermon would give much more detail, but I think you get the point. Many have received comfort and encouragement from these verses. The question remains; is that really what Jesus was talking about? The answer is yes and no. Remember, He was speaking on two levels.

Consider the Cultural Context

The aspiration of every Hebrew boy was to become a rabbi.

Unlike today, you didn't just go to school, turn 18 and enroll in rabbinical school. Training started as soon as the young boy was old enough to understand.

As written in the 12th century *Mishnah Torah,* by Rabbi Moses Maimonides, "Every person in Israel is obligated to be engaged in Torah learning, whether one is poor or wealthy, whether one is whole in body or afflicted with suffering, whether one is young or one is old and feeble, even a poor person who is supported by charity and goes from door to door seeking benevolence, even the man supporting his wife and children—everyone is required to find a set time during the day and night to study Torah, as it was said 'you shall go over it, again and again, day and night' (Joshua 1:8)."

Before becoming a Rabbi there were at least three stages:

Stage One:

Every Hebrew boy had to memorize Leviticus. This training was usually supervised by his father. We might call this his preschool education. At age six he would be tested. Memorization was the only way they could learn Scripture. Today most homes have multiple copies of the Bible, but in those days, the average Jewish home did not possess a single copy of the Torah. The father would teach his son from memory, the same way he was taught by his father.

If the young boy failed to successfully memorize Leviticus, he would be forever assigned to take up the profession of his father. More than likely he would become a fisherman or a carpenter. Those were the popular trades of the day. It's also true that he would be illiterate, unable to read or write, schooling for him would be over. It doesn't seem fair but that was the culture. At each level of learning you had to demonstrate that you were ready to progress to the next stage. Only the very best would be allowed to move forward.

Stage Two:

Even if he passed stage one, there was still no guarantee of going on for further training. If he was selected as one of the best of the best he would be enrolled in the "Bet Safar" or, "The School of the Torah." From ages 6 through 12 he would attend what we would call elementary school. At this stage the young boy would be taught by the rabbis. The scope of the teaching would include the Torah, or the first five books of the Bible. The rabbis were passing along what they had been taught and it was their assignment to perpetuate the traditional and accepted interpretation of the law.

Age 12 was the critical year. In order to graduate to the next level he would have to be selected in the highest group. Next, he would have to demonstrate to the rabbis an understanding of the first five books of the Torah. Not only did he have to memorize them, he had to have a working knowledge of what they meant.

The rabbis were not interested in perfect memorization. What elevated you to a higher plateau was if you could astound the teachers. How did a student do that? By knowing the right questions to ask in order to keep the discussion about God continuing. You see, it was the duty of the rabbi not to interpret the law but to keep the conversation about Yahweh in front of the people. It's important to note only the brightest students were invited to stand before the rabbis.

Question? Where was Jesus at age 12? He was at His graduation exam. He was in the temple astounding the teachers, and the rabbis were amazed at His knowledge. He was asking them questions for which they did not know the answers, and they were overwhelmed at His understanding of the Torah. I'm sure they whispered among themselves, "We have never encountered a young man like this one."

After three days they found him in the temple courts, sitting among the teachers, listening to them and asking them questions. Everyone who heard him was amazed at his understanding and his answers. When his parents saw him, they were astonished. His mother said to him, "Son, why have you treated us like this? Your father and I have been anxiously searching for you."

"Why were you searching for me?" he asked. "Didn't you know I had to be in my Father's house?" But they did not understand what he was saying to them (Luke 2:46-50 NIV).

Stage Three:

In the pages of Scripture, Jesus was not heard from between age 12 and 30. Why? He was attending rabbinical school, known as Bet Talmud—"The School of the Disciple." It is also referred to as Bet Midrash. Only the sharpest students made the cut. At any point, if a young man failed to make the grade, he was told to return and take up the occupation of his father. The selection process at this juncture was so intense that only a handful moved to ordination as rabbi.

There were five levels of the Bet Talmud. If the student completed the first four he was qualified as a rabbi. Jesus passed the test of the first level, and moved to the second, third, and fourth. At age 30 He passed the final test and could officially be called, Rabbi Jesus.

WHAT HISTORY TELLS US

The following facts are from *Jesus the Jewish Theologian,* by Brad H. Young, and *Sitting at the Feet of Rabbi Jesus,* by Ann Spangler and Lois Tverberg.

The word "rabbi" (or ravi) means "respected teacher" when roughly translated to English. But it is a rich, Hebrew concept that means much more. In the modern parlance, a rabbi is seen as the leader of a Jewish synagogue, but in the first century, prior to the fall of Jerusalem in 70 A.D., the title "rabbi" meant something much different.

After the Maccabean Revolt in the second century BC, a large number (more than 100,000) diaspora Jews from Babylon returned, en masse, over a short period of time back to the land of Israel, because it was now free of its enslavement by the Greeks.

Being as the land in Judea was largely settled, they chose the less favorable property around the Sea of Galilee and the Jezreel valley in which to settle.

These people were often called the *hasidim* ("the pious ones"), because of their exceeding fervor for worshiping God and keeping all of the Hebrew Scriptures (which we call the "Old Testament"). In contrast, the Jews living in Judea were much more secular and ceremonial—keeping only the Torah (Genesis through Deuteronomy) and maintaining the priesthood and Temple rites.

The hasidim brought with them the tradition of synagogue—a meeting place where all the gatherings of community life happened: studying Scripture, weddings, debates, festivals, and worship. Among the hasidim, there were a number of teachers, who were responsible for instructing the people on the Scriptures, primarily the children—most of whom would have the entire Torah memorized by the age of 12 (which is still the case in many hasidic communities in Israel).

These rabbis were not religious leaders or the keepers of the synagogue. Rather, they were seen as exactly what their name implied—a "respected teacher".

From the biblical record, we have note of seven different groups/types of people who refer to Jesus as "Rabbi" or "Teacher" (the rough translation): His disciples (Mark 9:5; Mark 11:21 etc.); Pharisees (John 3:1-2); John the Baptist's disciples (John 1:35-38); Common people (Mark 10:51; John 6:24-25); Torah teachers (Matthew 8:19); Herodians (Luke 3:12); and the Sadducees (Matthew 22:23-32). Additionally, Jesus refers to Himself by this title (John 13:12-14; Luke 22:10-11).

Jesus was not called Rabbi because He was just a teacher; there were a multitude of teachers in His day. He was given this title because He was qualified. He would have never been allowed to teach in the synagogue if He were not totally approved to do so.

> *Jesus returned to Galilee in the power of the Spirit, and news about him spread through the whole countryside. He was teaching in their synagogues, and everyone praised him.*

He went to Nazareth, where he had been brought up, and on the Sabbath day he went into the synagogue, as was his custom. He stood up to read, and the scroll of the prophet Isaiah was handed to him.

Unrolling it, he found the place where it is written: "The Spirit of the Lord is on me, because he has anointed me to proclaim good news to the poor. He has sent me to proclaim freedom for the prisoners and recovery of sight for the blind, to set the oppressed free, to proclaim the year of the Lord's favor."

Then he rolled up the scroll, gave it back to the attendant and sat down. The eyes of everyone in the synagogue were fastened on him. He began by saying to them, "Today this scripture is fulfilled in your hearing" (Luke 4:14-21 NIV).

They killed Jesus because He claimed to be God, but they called Him Rabbi because He earned it. He wasn't called a carpenter, rather "the son of a carpenter." The Pharisees would have never referred to Him as Rabbi if they thought he hadn't earned the title.

There was one final step the majority of rabbinical students would never attain. To put it in today's language you would have about as much an opportunity to reach the next level of authority as you would to play professional sports in our day!

For example, a recent statistical report by the NCAA says: "Basketball and football, the most visible of high school and college sports, have a very low percentage of athletes who play in high school and then eventually move up to the professional ranks. In men's basketball, for example, there is only a .03% chance of a pro career. This means that of the almost 156,000 male, high school senior basketball players only 44 will be drafted to play in the NBA after college, and only 32 women (.02%) out of just over 127,000 female, high school senior players will eventually be drafted. In football the odds are slightly better, with .08% or 250 of just over 317,000 high school senior players being drafted." I think you get the point!

The level I'm referring to in Jesus' time is a rabbi with

"Semicha." Only one or two rabbis qualify at the next level (maybe) every one hundred years. Semicha literally means "a rabbi with authority." Only the very highest student graduated with such honor. Why was it important for a rabbi to have this designation? If you didn't have authority or Semicha, all you could do is simply repeat what the rabbis taught you. You were not allowed to teach from your own interpretation of the Torah. Just a rabbi with Semicha could interpret the law.

As biblical scholar Brad Young points out:

> *The title "Rabbi", in first-century contemporary literature, could refer both to Torah teachers ("Teachers of the Law") and sages, rabbis with Semicha (authority). Jesus, who was clearly recognized by this title, would have fallen into one of these two categories, though clearly— from Scripture—it was the latter.*
>
> *Among these scholars were a very small subset, who were seen as having Semicha (authority). This Semicha allowed them to make new interpretations on how to live out Torah. (It is important to note that even they could not change Torah, but that their interpretation was on how to view it correctly so as to know how to live and act correctly, so as to please God.) Among these rabbis with Semicha, prior to the first century A.D., we know several names, with Honi and Hillel (the grandfather of Paul's rabbi, Gamaliel—who was quite famous, in his own right) as the most prominent in this timeframe. (These Semicha rabbis are often denoted by scholars as "sages", whereas Scripture refers to the rabbis without Semicha as Torah Teachers (Teachers of the Law).*
>
> *These Semicha rabbis were also unique, because they lived a more itinerant lifestyle and took on followers —called talmidim (disciples)—who lived with them most of the time, though they would be sent out on their own later in their learning. The rabbis had a yoke, their method of interpreting Scripture, in which they would order the commandments of Torah from greatest to least. The*

talmidim of a rabbi would be expected to live by that yoke and to memorize the key teachings of that rabbi. Living with their rabbi, these talmidim would also learn to live in the same manner—with their greatest desire to be to learn to follow God just like their rabbi. In all of this, the talmidim were also in complete submission to the authority of their rabbi.

At the age of 30, those who graduated from rabbinical school were baptized. The Jewish culture baptized for everything, including when you graduated from elementary school. Then at every level of progression, baptism was the seal of approval.

At the time of Jesus there were two rabbis with Semicha; Hallel and Shamai. They both died when Jesus was about 18. So, from the year when Jesus was 18 until He was 30, all of Israel was waiting for the next rabbi with Semicha. Upon graduation from rabbinical school, Jesus was baptized.

To be recognized as a rabbi with Semicha, two witnesses were necessary to testify to the supernatural power of God on that person's life.

According to Hebrew tradition, for a sage-rabbi to have Semicha—authority to make new teachings to interpret Scripture—he had to be acknowledged as a prophet from God, himself. Or, just as Aaron and Moses had given authority to 70 elders, they had to be recognized as having Semicha by two other rabbis with Semicha.

Enter witness #1 – John the Baptist

We know from the Scriptures that John the Baptist was considered to be a similar sort of rabbi (John 3:26) or a prophet (Matthew 11:7-9), with disciples of his own (Matthew 9:14), and followers in Asia Minor, who were later baptized into Jesus by Paul (Acts 19:1-7).

As we read in John 1:29-34 NIV:

The next day John saw Jesus coming toward him and said, "Look, the Lamb of God, who takes away the sin of the world! This is the one I meant when I said, 'A man who comes after me has surpassed me because he was before me.' I myself did not know him, but the reason I came baptizing with water was that he might be revealed to Israel."

Then John gave this testimony: "I saw the Spirit come down from heaven as a dove and remain on him. And I myself did not know him, but the one who sent me to baptize with water told me, 'The man on whom you see the Spirit come down and remain is the one who will baptize with the Holy Spirit.' I have seen and I testify that this is God's Chosen One."

Additionally, when Jesus was questioned by the Sadducees as to where He received His Semicha (authority), His answer (according to the rabbinic technique of answering in questions) would indicate that John, a prophet had heralded (not granted) His authority from God.

John was the forerunner of a new covenant. He was a transition man, one who had been blowing up their religious system. This "wild prophet," crying from the wilderness, "Behold the Lamb of God who takes away the sin of the world," was bearing witness that Jesus was more than just an ordinary teacher. When Jesus came up out of the water, He was ordained a traditional rabbi, but that's not the end of the story.

Enter witness #2 – God the Father

"As soon as Jesus was baptized, he went up out of the water. At that moment heaven was opened, and he saw the Spirit of God descending like a dove and alighting on him. And a voice from heaven said, 'This is my Son, whom I love; with him I am well pleased'" (Matthew 3:16-17 NIV).

When Jesus was challenged about His authority, He simply reminded them of what happened at His baptism. He would point them to John, the dove, and the voice from heaven that resounded throughout Israel! They had no answer for that because they were witnesses to the events. Jesus told them, *"I only do what the Father tells me to do and I only say what the Father tells me to say."*

Jesus didn't answer to the high priest, He answered to His heavenly Father, and they hated Him even more. They knew He was no ordinary rabbi, He was one with Semicha. God's Son fulfilled everything the law required of a rabbi with this designation:

- He had a yoke (Matthew 11:28-30; 22:36-40).
- He sent out His disciples on their own later in their learning (Matthew 10:5-25).
- They memorized His teaching and followed it (Matthew 7:24-29; Luke 6:46-49).
- They lived with Him so that they could follow His example (Matthew 10:1, 16:24-28).

WHY WAS JESUS SO POPULAR?

When a rabbi had authority (Semicha), He made his own context of teaching or interpretation of the Torah and it was called his *yoke*. That is why Jesus said, *"Take My yoke upon you and learn from Me...For My yoke is easy and My burden is light"* (Matthew 11:29-30).

Jesus was referring to much more than we have understood. He was not simply talking about a team of oxen wearing a heavy yoke, even though it is a picture of religious oppression. He was simply letting the world know that His yoke (interpretation of the law) is easy and His burden is light. You have heard generations of teachings from rabbis telling you could never measure up, but Jesus was declaring that there was a better way to live.

If you ever wondered why Jesus was so popular and could draw crowds of thousands to hear His teachings, the answer is simple: He was a Rabbi with authority (Semicha). The people were hungry for spiritual leadership, and were amazed how Jesus wrecked all the yokes of the religious leaders of His day because *"He taught them as one having authority, and not as the scribes"* (Mark 1:22).

They didn't flock to Him because He could feed them or work miracles. They were hungry, not for food, but for a fresh word from heaven. The people were learning that they could actually have a relationship with God. No longer did they have to feel displaced and unqualified.

Those who were wearing the yoke of religion, were waiting and hoping for someone to lift it from their shoulders. Their whole life they were taught rules and regulations. They knew they didn't qualify and would never be good enough to meet the standards laid down by the religious authorities. They were in a hopeless and helpless situation. Oppressed by the Romans and condemned by their religion, they were living in a world of darkness.

Like a bolt of lightning, Jesus steps onto the stage of history and declared, *"My yoke is easy, and My burden is light."* Immediately, they knew His teaching was different from the other rabbis. They were hearing things they had never heard before and something stirred in their hearts. Jesus knew that religion was based on fear and guilt, so He didn't step down from heaven to start a new religion! No, a thousand times no! He came to offer a new and better way, and He had the authority (Semicha) to back it up.

The Pharisees didn't know what to do with Jesus. Not because He had a following or worked miracles, because they dealt with religious zealots all the time. There were many in that day who made all kinds of messianic claims. If for one minute they thought Jesus was just another fraud they would not have bothered with Him. Here was a rabbi who spoke with authority (Semicha) and claimed to be God. The story of His baptism spread like wildfire throughout the land. While they refused to recognize Jesus as the Son of God, they could not deny that He was a rabbi with authority.

They didn't bring Jesus to trial on the accusation that He fed thousands of people with a small lunch of five loaves and two fish. It was because He had the unmitigated gall to say to a lame man, "Your sins are forgiven you." With scorn in their voices they chided, "Only God can forgive sin—how dare you!" Time and again, as they listened to Jesus teach, they knew He had to be stopped.

A Rabbi Needs Disciples

In a recent sermon Pastor Charles Henrickson made this statement:

> *Jesus takes the initiative and calls the disciples. In many respects the circle of disciples gathered about Jesus was no startling novelty in first-century Palestine: In the terminology of 'rabbi' and 'disciple,' in the fact that they 'followed' their Master. But in this point, in the genesis of the circle of disciples, there is a striking difference. In rabbinical circles the initiative in discipleship lay with the disciple. 'Take to yourself a teacher,' is the advice given to the aspiring disciple by a Jewish teacher. We have no record of a call issued by a Jewish rabbi to a disciple in all rabbinic literature. What in Judaism was the pious duty of the disciple is here the sovereign act of the Master. Jesus reserves the initiative for Himself.*
>
> *As with those first disciples, so also with us, Jesus' disciples today. We didn't seek him. He sought us, and found us, and called us to be His own. Jesus said He came to seek and to save the lost. That was us. We were lost, lost in our sin and darkness, and we didn't even know it. Like those first disciples, like all the lost people in the world today, we were just going about our everyday business, casting our nets and mending our nets, but unable to mend our relationship with God. That net was torn beyond repair, and we couldn't fix it. That's what it means to be lost, lost in sin and heading toward death, eternal death apart from God.*
>
> *But then Jesus comes walking. He sees us, He finds us where we are. He speaks to us, words of life and forgiveness, because it is the call to come and follow Him. Jesus calls us in the gospel. He called you in your baptism, when you didn't do a thing to choose Him. You were dead, and He brought you to life. You didn't decide to follow Jesus. He chose to call you.*

Where would a rabbi gather disciples? At the school of disciples—the Bet Talmud. Here, the rabbi would select a group of newly ordained and baptized 12-year-old boys. It would be his responsibility to teach them from age 12 to age 30. The number one requirement for choosing his disciples would be that the rabbi believed they could do greater works than himself. So the cycle continued to repeat itself. A rabbi without disciples would be equivalent to a college professor teaching to an empty classroom.

However, Jesus didn't go to the school of the disciples (the Bet Talmud) to call those who would follow Him. He went to the lake. Without a doubt, the men in those boats knew exactly who He was. All their life they heard, "Not good enough. Not qualified. Failure." But along came Jesus, who said two simple words that changed everything, "Follow Me!"

As it has been said, "Jesus didn't call the qualified, He qualified the called." These men would not have been on anyone's list to become disciples. Tradition says that because of a lack of education—more than likely they could not read or write—their destiny was sealed on a fishing boat. On more than one occasion Jesus was accused of allowing ignorant and unlearned men to follow Him. *"Now as they observed the confidence of Peter and John and understood that they were uneducated and untrained men, they were amazed, and began to recognize them as having been with Jesus"* (Acts 4:13 NIV).

Religion had wrapped its yoke around their neck and said, "You are unqualified, hopeless, and helpless because you can never meet the standards of our religion." But Jesus didn't look at what they were, He saw what they would become. Is it any wonder they dropped everything to follow Him? This was their opportunity at a second chance. He wrapped His yoke around the neck of the downtrodden, those without hope, and said, "Follow Me. My yoke is easy."

JESUS LOVES TO TAKE NOBODIES AND MAKE THEM SOMEBODIES!

"Brothers and sisters, think of what you were when you were

called. Not many of you were wise by human standards; not many were influential; not many were of noble birth. But God chose the foolish things of the world to shame the wise; God chose the weak things of the world to shame the strong. God chose the lowly things of this world and the despised things—and the things that are not—to nullify the things that are, so that no one may boast before him. It is because of him that you are in Christ Jesus, who has become for us wisdom from God—that is, our righteousness, holiness and redemption. Therefore, as it is written: 'Let the one who boasts boast in the Lord'" (1 Corinthians 1:26-31 NIV).

I am thankful for every prominent Christian who witnesses for the Lord—grateful for the All-American football player who uses his athletic ability to point people to Christ, and for the beauty queen who states publicly that she is a Christian. But God gives testimonies to *all* His children.

According to the above passage, God chooses to use all manner of people, regardless of their weaknesses or their strengths, their talents or their lack of ability. That promise includes you and me. We may never be elected president of our class, win an award, or become famous for our brilliance. But no matter who we are, God can use us! The Bible is filled with examples of the Lord picking nobodies and using them to bring Glory to His Name.

Who was Noah?

Was he a great man who everyone looked up to and revered? Noah was a "nobody" who was never heard about until the time God was preparing to destroy the face of the earth with a devastating flood. Why did the Almighty choose Noah to build the ark? Was there something special about him? Why didn't God choose someone else?

Who was Abram?

What was so unique about Abram that God would call him out of all the people that were living at the time? Why didn't the Lord select someone else instead?

Let's look at some other "nobodies" who the Lord transformed into "somebodies":

- Joseph
- Moses
- Joshua
- Samson
- Gideon
- David
- Solomon

Now, add your name to the list!

Over and over again, God astounds and amazes us with those He chooses to use. In the Bible, and elsewhere in human history, God confounds the world with the very things it considers to be foolish, even stupid. Paul said that *"the message of the cross is foolishness to those who are perishing"* (1 Corinthians 1:18).

So, if the world considers the Gospel message to be foolish, then it must be true that God's messengers are considered to be fools.

A DIVINE CHAIN OF EVENTS

A nobody by the name of Edward Kimball heard the call to follow Jesus and started a chain reaction of events that changed the course of modern history.

As recorded by Lyle Dorsett, in his book, *A Passion for Souls: The Life of Dwight L. Moody,* one afternoon Mr. Kimball stopped by a shoe store where a young man, D. L. Moody, was working. After a brief conversation Mr. Kimball led him to faith in Jesus Christ.

Moody started a Sunday school, began to share his faith, became an evangelist, went to England, and eventually was invited to preach to the congregation of the most famous scholar of his time, Dr. F. B. Meyer.

When Moody began preaching that morning, Dr. Meyer thought, "Oh, my, what have I done? Moody's language is atrocious, and my dignified congregation will be embarrassed and humiliated by his terrible speaking." Yet, when the service was over, he saw tears running down the face of one of the finest ladies in his congregation. "Dear lady," Dr. Meyer said, "what's your reaction to Mr. Moody?" She smiled and replied, "Oh, Dr. Meyer, my heart hasn't been so moved and touched in years as that man touched me today."

That morning Dr. Meyer learned something about the language of the soul and God changed his ministry.

Eventually Dr. Meyer came to the United States to preach and an American evangelist by the name of Wilbur Chapman was touched by his teaching. Chapman had a young, recently converted baseball player by the name of Billy Sunday as his assistant. He eventually turned over his evangelistic responsibilities to him.

Billy Sunday was invited to preach a revival in Charlotte, North Carolina, in 1924. A men's prayer and fellowship group, originally known as the Billy Sunday Layman's Evangelistic Club and later renamed as Charlotte Businessmen's Club (CBMC), grew out of those meetings. This group of men began to pray that God would do even greater things in their city. As a result of their prayers, an evangelist by the name of Mordecai Ham came to Charlotte in 1934 to preach. During these meetings a "nobody" of a boy at 17 years of age placed his faith in Christ and was born again into the family of God.

You know of this man who grew up to go to college and become a well-known evangelist, radio and television speaker and advisor to presidents. His name is Billy Graham. He has proclaimed the Gospel to more people than any other man in world history. A nobody became somebody!

And so it is with people like you and me. Jesus has come to transform the ordinary into the extraordinary. He has come not for greatness, but for sinners like us.

Why does God use nobodies? Paul explains it this way, that *"no flesh should glory in His presence"* (1 Corinthians 1:29).

Suppose, for example, the children of Israel had sent a giant of their own to fight Goliath and the Philistine had lost? The Israelites would have started bragging about their giant and not God's supernatural power. But when the Lord took a young shepherd boy and used him to defeat the giant, God received all the glory.

Without a doubt, when we reach heaven, the Almighty won't let us brag about how we got there. We will not be able to say, "My brains did it; my strength did it; my social standing did it."

When we are standing before Jesus, God's nobodies are going to be as highly praised as anyone we might think of as wise, mighty, or noble. When twelve unqualified, unlearned men answered the call to follow Jesus, the course of human history was set on a path of redemption. From the Sea of Galilee to wherever you personally answered "Yes" to follow Him, you also were set on the road of greatness.

When the yoke of religion resounds, "No," the yoke of Jesus says, "Yes!"

CHAPTER 3

COVERED IN DUST

We need not climb up into heaven to see whether our sins are forgiven: let us look into our hearts, and see if we can forgive others. If we can, we need not doubt but God has forgiven us.

– THOMAS WATSON

Jesus, now qualified as a Rabbi with Semicha (authority),begins to teach his yoke. *"Come to Me, all you who labor and are heavy laden, and I will give you rest. Take My yoke upon you and learn from Me, for I am gentle and lowly in heart, and you will find rest for your souls. For My yoke is easy and My burden is light"* (Matthew 11:28-30).

For 18 years the people had waited for a rabbi with the authority to not only repeat the tradition of the rabbis who taught them, but someone with the authority to interpret the law with understanding. Remember, when Jesus said, *"Take My yoke upon you and learn from Me,"* He was referring to more than a team of oxen bearing a heavy yoke. The meaning included the body of His teaching (His yoke) and the interpretation of the law. His yoke provides a better way of life, which is key to His teachings in the New Testament.

In Hebrew tradition, each qualified rabbi would go to the Bet Talmud (or the school of disciples) to gather the 12 most competent young men and teach them for the next 18 years of their life. But Jesus was different. He went to the Sea of Galilee, stood on the shore, and called those who wouldn't normally be chosen. Professional fisherman were never considered for being a disciple of any rabbi—much less a rabbi with Semicha. Eventually 12 men of various backgrounds, who were unqualified, answered the call to follow Rabbi Jesus.

It is stated in rabbinical tradition that when a rabbi gathered his disciples, he wanted to teach them how to talk like him, teach like him, even walk like him. It is said that he would tie a rope around their neck and they would follow in a straight line, trying to copy their teacher. According to Elyah Israel, in *The Hebrew Bible is the Mind of God*, the rabbi was teaching them to walk in *ahad*—a word that signifies unity, singularity, and togetherness. It's what Jesus prayed for in John 17, that His disciples would walk in one accord—or *ahad*.

Eventually, the Jewish rabbi would take the rope off of his students. If one of them strayed off course, the others would bring the disciple back into line. Perhaps Jesus was referring to this tradition when He told the parable of the lost sheep, lost silver, and lost son. (See Luke 15.)

It is also stated in Jewish tradition that on the streets, the best student of the day would walk directly behind the rabbi. It's much like the ones in elementary school who receive gold stars by their name for doing all the right things.

In the first century, the reward was being able to walk close behind the teacher. When the line leader would return to school, the dust of the rabbi would cover him from the waist down. However, there was no way the student was going to wash off the dust; it was a badge of honor! When he returned to the Bet Talmud, he wanted all the other students to see the dust and know he was special.

We need to ask: are we covered in the dust of Rabbi Jesus? Tragically our churches are filled with people who are coated in the wrong dust.

Some are covered in denominational pride.

It makes no difference whether it's Baptist dust, Methodist dust, Pentecostal dust, or any other doctrine which has enveloped man with its own traditions and biases. Denominational dust says, "We are right and everybody else is wrong."

It's scary to think some church organizations can be so filled with pride that they will tell its people not to read or listen to certain teachers who may not agree with the denominational tradition. Dust is dust, no matter the name! Jesus said, *"Thus you nullify the word of God for the sake of your tradition"* (Matthew 15:6 NIV).

Some are covered in comparative theology.

This dust means that we want mercy and grace for ourselves, but judgment and condemnation for others. Comparative theology magnifies the sins of others and minimizes our own. I compare myself with you and always come out on top! Have you ever noticed those covered with this dust love to discuss the sins of others masked under the disguise of "concern"?

Some are covered in personal preferences.

This dust places preferences above the Word of God. I can remember a time when the established church went through the "Worship Wars." Churches have split apart over music styles. The debate raged over hymn books, overhead projectors, and choir robes. Depending on which side you were on, your personal taste dictated how you would fight. If you thought singing out of the hymn book was more spiritual than looking on a big screen with the words of choruses, then you defended to the death your viewpoint. On the other hand, if you thought that choruses and up-to-date music was the style, of course you defended that position. Every church had "turf shepherds and power players," who believed it was their duty to protect and defend the established traditions, and nothing—and no one—was going to change it without their approval.

The funny thing is, nobody stopped long enough to ask what God thought about it! I once heard of a lady who walked up to the pastor after a service. This church happened to be singing more modern music mixed with the old. She complained, "I don't like this new stuff, we need to stick to the traditional music!" The pastor replied, "I'm so sorry you don't like the new music, but we didn't sing it for you, we sang it for God, and He loved it!"

Worship is a matter of the heart, not a hymn book or an overhead projector. You can sing with or without a hymnal, or even write the words on the back of your hand. What really matters is whether or not your heart is worshiping the Lord. Jesus spoke of those who *"honor Me with their lips, but their heart is far from Me"* (Matthew 15:8).

The dust of the modern church has spread like a blanket across cities, small towns, and communities around the world. No wonder people are confused. The same individuals the church is so desperate to reach has to wonder why there is a church on every corner and we can't seem to get it together. Instead of changing the culture, it seems the church has been changed *by* the culture. Instead of declaring a better way of life, the church shouts to the world, "Join us and we will teach you *our* way of life—which includes all of our own rules and regulations and interpretations of Scripture."

It's not that I'm against the church, not at all. I'm concerned what we have done to her. The Apostle Paul counseled:

> *Husbands, love your wives, just as Christ also loved the church and gave Himself for her, that He might sanctify and cleanse her with the washing of water by the word, that He might present her to Himself a glorious church, not having spot or wrinkle or any such thing, but that she should be holy and without blemish. So husbands ought to love their own wives as their own bodies; he who loves his wife loves himself. For no one ever hated his own flesh, but nourishes and cherishes it, just as the Lord does the church* (Ephesians 5:25-29).

We are told to be salt and light, wise as serpents and harmless as doves. Tragically, we have turned that into a lightweight, minimum-impact, watered-down church that has no effect on today's culture. The house of God has become a thermometer (registers the temperature) instead of thermostats (regulates the temperature). A thermometer will tell you exactly what the temperature is, but a thermostat will tell you what it's going to be based on the instructions you give it.

In Acts 17, Paul and his team were in Thessalonica, where they were accused of being troublemakers. Why? For preaching a new religion? For condemning the city? No, actually they were only there for a short period of time and yet a riot broke out. They were not proclaiming a new kind of religion. Rather, they were declaring there was one King and His name was not Caesar! His name was Jesus. The issue was not about religion, they had plenty of gods for that. What got them in trouble was declaring "another king."

In that day, revering Caesar was the highest form of worship. He represented the state, and the state was the king—therefore, whoever was the "Caesar" at the time would be worshiped as the supreme god. The "purists" would go to the temple and worship Mars or Venus, but when it came to the real issues of life, culture, and the economy, the state knows best. Neptune may get your sacrifice and incense of worship, but Caesar got your taxes!

The yoke of Rabbi Jesus is not one of a new religion. He came to declare the kingdom of God!

There was a time when the local church was the center of influence in the city. To see how things have changed, look around on Sunday morning and notice the difference. Instead of King Jesus, we have king pleasure, sports, shopping, and all other activities you would see on a normal day. There's nothing wrong with any of those pursuits, but I am old enough to remember the day when no activities would be scheduled during the worship hour on Sunday morning.

TWO KINGDOMS IN CONFLICT

The dust (yoke) of Rabbi Jesus speaks of a better way of life. He was constantly running against the stone wall of the yoke of religion. At every turn, at every teaching, there were two main groups who were opposing Him. To better understand why there was such resistance, we need to know who they were and what Jesus thought about them.

In Matthew 16:11-12, we read, *"'How is it you do not understand that I did not speak to you concerning bread?—but to beware of the <u>leaven of the Pharisees and Sadducees.</u>' Then they understood that He did not tell them to beware of the leaven of bread, but of the doctrine of the Pharisees and Sadducees."*

Luke 12:1-3 records, *"In the meantime, when an innumerable multitude of people had gathered together, so that they trampled one another, He began to say to His disciples first of all, 'Beware of the leaven of the Pharisees, which is hypocrisy. For there is nothing covered that will not be revealed, nor hidden that will not be known. Therefore whatever you have spoken in the dark will be heard in the light, and what you have spoken in the ear in inner rooms will be proclaimed on the housetops.'"*

It took a while for Jesus to convince His disciples that He was not talking to them about physical leaven, but about a spiritual truth. He often used the natural to illustrate the spiritual.

First the Natural:

Leaven—zume (dzoo'-may); probably ferment (as if boiling up): 1. An agent, such as yeast, that causes batter or dough to rise, especially by fermentation. 2. An element, influence, or agent that works subtly to lighten, enliven, or modify a whole.

Now the spiritual:

Leaven (yeast) and teaching resemble each other in several respects: Both operate invisibly, are very potent, and have a tendency gradually to augment their sphere of influence.

We are all products of who teaches us.

The dust of religion was spread by the Pharisees and the Sadducees. In order to understand the importance of their influence let me share a a brief history lesson.

1. The Pharisees

Of the two groups, the Pharisees were the most prominent. They arrived on the scene during the last half of the first century BC and continued until the destruction of Jerusalem by Rome in AD 70. The word Pharisee means, "One who is separated." The name for this Jewish sect most likely comes from their reading of two important texts in the Law of Moses. The first is Leviticus 11:44, where God declares, *"You shall be holy; for I am holy."* The rabbis interpreted that to mean, *"As I am a separated one, so should you be separated ones."*

The second text which calls for separation is Exodus 19:6,

where God says the Israelites were to be a kingdom of priests and a holy nation. The rabbis interpreted that to mean, "Holy, hallowed, separated from the peoples of the world and their detestable things."

Because of their great emphasis on external holiness and separation, the Pharisees stressed the Old Testament purity laws: tithing, fasting, prayer, and by all means separation from everyone and everything ceremonially unclean. The thing that most distinguished the Pharisees from everyone else was their allegiance to the Halakah, the oral law. The Halakah, according to the Pharisees, contained laws that God gave Moses on Mount Sinai, which Moses did not write down. They were preserved orally and handed down from one generation to the next by scribes and experts in the law who memorized them. To the Pharisees, the oral traditions were just as binding as the written text of Scripture.

We gain much information about the Pharisees' practices from both the New Testament and from Jewish historian Josephus. He tells us that the Pharisees were "the most accurate exegetes of the law." Many of them were priests. They were the professors of the day and tied to the famous school of Hillel. They were not as interested in politics as they were religion, but they were very much opposed to cooperation with Rome. They believed Israel to be God's sovereign nation and should only be ruled by Him alone. They refused to take an oath of loyalty to Herod the Great and the Roman government.

Because the Pharisees were so popular with the people, Herod did not retaliate against them. They wielded the greatest influence on religious thinking and practice in that day, so it is no surprise that they appear about one hundred times in the New Testament.

2. The Sadducees

Another group came onto the scene during the last half of the first century BC and became extinct in AD 7—the Sadducees. There are several possibilities as to what their name means. One likely suggestion is that Sadducees is a derivative from the Hebrew word *tsadik* which means "righteous one." Another view is that they are named after a famous priest during the reigns of David and Solomon named Zadok, making Sadducee equivalent to Zadokite. If this is true, then the Sadducees would be making a claim about their authority to serve as priests and most especially that the High Priest be a Sadducee.

The Sadducees were more interested in politics than were their Pharisaical counterparts. The Sadducees had power and held the majority in the Sanhedrin, the Jewish Religious Supreme Court. They had control of the high priesthood and discharged most of the duties at the Temple. So they were interested in keeping the status quo.

They were inclined to cooperate with Herod the Great and the Romans. This group also felt threatened by any popular movement, especially if it had political overtones. So when Jesus gained a large following, claiming to be King over God's kingdom, the Sadducees saw Him as a serious threat.

They are mentioned by name only 14 times in the New Testament. From these texts, together with Josephus, we can get a rather good description of the Sadducees. They were more aristocratic and tended to be wealthy, rural landowners. They had a reputation for being ruthless and murderous. Just look at how they treated Christ at His trial. They bribed false witnesses, they beat Him, spat upon Him, mocked and cursed Him, etc. Acts 23 shows us they took an oath to murder the Apostle Paul.

The Sadducees were an arrogant lot who, according to John the Baptist, placed their trust in their ancestry. They were clearly much more politicians than priests, though they insisted that theirs, not the Pharisees', was the prerogative for interpreting the Law of Moses. The Sadducees were very legalistic and rejected the oral law of the Pharisees, and are perhaps best remembered today for their disbelief in the resurrection and afterlife. Being wealthy and power hungry, they were more focused on this world and more worldly-minded than spiritually-minded.

With this abbreviated historical overview of the Pharisees and Sadducees, let's return to our text in Matthew 16, where Jesus says, *"Be on your guard against the yeast of the Pharisees and Sadducees."* What was Jesus telling us? Better yet, what is He saying to you and me today? Is this yeast of the Pharisees and Sadducees still a threat? Whose dust are you covered in?

THE SAME RELIGIOUS SPIRIT IS AT WORK TODAY

Based upon what we know about these two groups from the New Testament and other historical sources, here are a few specks of their yeast that still threaten to work its way through the church and destroy it.

1. Self-Righteousness

"Everything they do is done for men to see: They make their phylacteries wide and the tassels on their garments long; they love the place of honor at banquets and the most important seats in the synagogues; they love to be greeted in the marketplaces and to have men call them `Rabbi.'" (Matthew 23: 5-7NIV).

I have no doubt that if the Pharisees and Sadducees were still around today they would wear the collars turned around and flowing clerical robes, not only when they preached, but when they went to the market.

Jesus was the opposite of these men. I love the story of a little six-year-old girl who suddenly looked up at her mom and remarked, "Mother, I think Jesus was the only one who ever dared to live His life inside out!" The mother was fairly dazed by her young daughter's thought, but the girl might be right. She had heard His story and knew He was so pure in His soul that there was nothing that He needed to conceal from anybody. Jesus was the only one in the history of mankind of whom that could be truly said.

2. Judgmental Spirit

A Pharisee by the name of Simon asked Jesus to come to his home for a meal. This is where a woman washed His feet with her tears.

"When the Pharisee who had invited him saw this, he said to himself, "If this man were a prophet, he would know who is touching him and what kind of woman she is—that she is a sinner" (Luke 7:39 NIV).

Instead of seeing a person with a broken and contrite heart, or someone falling at the feet of Jesus for mercy and compassion, Simon saw "a sinner!"

An example of this is found in a parable Jesus told to those who trusted in themselves, thinking they were righteous, yet they despised others.

> *Two men went up to the temple to pray, one a Pharisee and the other a tax collector. The Pharisee stood and prayed thus with himself, "God, I thank you that I am not like other men—extortioners, unjust, adulterers, or even as this tax collector. I fast twice a week; I give tithes of all that I possess."*
>
> *And the tax collector, standing afar off, would not so much as raise his eyes to heaven, but beat his breast, saying, "God, be merciful to me a sinner!" I tell you, this man went down to his house justified rather than the other; for everyone who exalts himself will be humbled, and he who humbles himself will be exalted* (Luke 18:9-14 NIV).

3. Rigid Legalism

Both the Pharisees and Sadducees operated out of a rigid legalistic philosophy. The law was the law and that was that. Therefore, when Jesus healed on the Sabbath, they refused to praise God or rejoice with those who were healed. As far as they were concerned, Jesus broke the law, and the law is all that mattered.

> *Now He was teaching in one of the synagogues on the Sabbath. And behold, there was a woman who had a spirit of infirmity eighteen years, and was bent over and could in no way raise herself up. But when Jesus saw her, He called her to Him and said to her, "Woman, you are loosed from your infirmity." And He laid His hands on her, and immediately she was made straight, and glorified God.*
>
> *But the ruler of the synagogue answered with indignation, because Jesus had healed on the Sabbath; and He said to the crowd, "There are six days on which men*

ought to work; therefore come and be healed on them, and not on the Sabbath day."

The Lord then answered him and said, "Hypocrite! Does not each one of you on the Sabbath loose his ox or donkey from the stall, and lead it away to water it? So ought not this woman, being a daughter of Abraham, whom Satan has bound—think of it—for eighteen years, be loosed from this bond on the Sabbath?"

And when He said these things, all His adversaries were put to shame; and all the multitude rejoiced for all the glorious things that were done by Him (Luke 13:10-17 NIV).

4. Bound By Tradition

Jesus didn't hesitate to confront these religious leaders. He told them, *"Isaiah was right when he prophesied about you hypocrites; as it is written: 'These people honor me with their lips, but their hearts are far from me. They worship Me in vain; their teachings are merely human rules'...Thus you nullify the word of God by your tradition that you have handed down. And you do many things like that"* (Mark 7:6-7,13 NIV).

Tradition is morally neutral, neither good nor bad. And it's something every church has. Even if you decide you will do things differently each Sunday and change your worship format for every service, well, that becomes your tradition. Since tradition is neither right, nor wrong, the problem surfaces when I bind my tradition on you, when I judge you because you do not do church "my way."

5. Self-Interest

After Jesus raised Lazarus from the dead, *"...many of the Jews who had come to visit Mary, and had seen what Jesus did, put their faith in him. But some of them went to the Pharisees and told them what Jesus had done. Then the chief priests and the Pharisees called a meeting of the Sanhedrin. 'What are we accomplishing?' they asked. 'Here is this man performing many miraculous signs. If we let him go on like this, everyone will believe in him, and then the Romans will come and take away both our place and our nation.'"* (John 11:45-48 NIV).

Please note the emphasis in this text. A mighty miracle has been performed. One who had been dead and in the tomb for four days has been raised to life. It was a time of great joy, wonder, and awe. But not for the Pharisees and Sadducees. They did not view Jesus' miracles in their best self-interest. They were jealous of Jesus and His popularity.

6. They Were Hypocrites, Teaching One Thing And Practicing Another.

Jesus called the Pharisees, *"Hypocrites!"* (Matthew 15:7), because their behavior did not match the laws they preached.

7. They Did Their Works To Be Seen And Appreciated By Men

> *Therefore whatever they tell you to observe, that observe and do, but do not do according to their works; for they say, and do not do. For they bind heavy burdens, hard to bear, and lay them on men's shoulders; but they themselves will not move them with one of their fingers. But all their works they do to be seen by men. They make their phylacteries broad and enlarge the borders of their garments. They love the best places at feasts, the best seats in the synagogues, greetings in the marketplaces, and to be called by men, "Rabbi, Rabbi." Jesus says, "Do as they say do, but not as they themselves do!"* (Matthew 23:3-7 NIV).

The problem is not with what they say they believe, but with their practice of their beliefs. At the heart of their hypocrisy was their love of honor. The Pharisees were more interested in gaining the approval and accolades of their fellow men than they were of God. Their religion had a motive, but it was not glorifying the Almighty, instead they had a desire for position, prominence and recognition.

They also liked to be called "rabbi," which was a title of respect given to teachers. It corresponds to the honorary title of Doctor given to preachers and teachers today. I don't have a problem calling someone "Doctor," but those who insist that everyone call them by that title may have an ego problem.

8. They Loved the Spotlight and Special Treatment, and They Endangered Souls

"But woe to you, scribes and Pharisees, hypocrites! For you shut up the kingdom of heaven against men; for you neither go in yourselves, nor do you allow those who are entering to go in" (Matthew 23:13 NIV).

The Pharisees and scribes would not associate themselves with Jesus and the truth He taught, and, by that rejection, they prevented others from coming to the truth because of their false teaching and their hypocritical lifestyles.

SINCE HYPOCRISY IS SOMETHING JESUS CONDEMNS, HOW CAN WE KEEP IT OUT OF OUR LIVES?

> *In the meantime, when an innumerable multitude of people had gathered together, so that they trampled one another, He began to say to His disciples first of all, "Beware of the leaven of the Pharisees, which is hypocrisy. For there is nothing covered that will not be revealed, nor hidden that will not be known. Therefore whatever you have spoken in the dark will be heard in the light, and what you have spoken in the ear in inner rooms will be proclaimed on the housetops.*
>
> *And I say to you, My friends, do not be afraid of those who kill the body, and after that have no more that they can do. But I will show you whom you should fear: Fear Him who, after He has killed, has power to cast into hell; yes, I say to you, fear Him! Are not five sparrows sold for two copper coins? And not one of them is forgotten before God. But the very hairs of your head are all numbered. Do not fear therefore; you are of more value than many sparrows* (Luke 12:1-7 NIV).

To keep hypocrisy out of our lives, we must first recognize

what it is. Jesus compared it to yeast or leaven, something every Jew would associate with sin and evil. The Apostle Paul also used leaven to symbolize sin when, in 1 Corinthians 5, he talked about church discipline and how if sin is not dealt with, it will work its way through the whole batch of dough.

Like yeast, hypocrisy starts very small but grows very quickly. And once a person begins to pretend who he or she is, the pretending increases to a point where the individual no longer knows who they are. They are always putting on a mask trying to be someone else.

One way to eliminate hypocrisy from our lives is not to gloss over it, but to uncover it for what it really is. To pretend is to lie—and to lie is to sin. According to Revelation 21:8, the eventual home of habitual liars will be the fiery lake of burning sulfur, the second death.

I read that in various places on earth there grows what has been named the Judas Tree—because of its deceitfulness. It has beautiful crimson blossoms that appear before the leaves sprout. These blossoms attract many insects, including bees. But every insect that lights upon these blossoms, eats a fatal opiate and drops dead. So beneath the Judas Tree are the remains of its victims.

This tree illustrates the deceitfulness and the danger of sin—which leads to death. We need to pray for guidance and wisdom to discern "Judas trees" that Satan has planted all around us.

Another way to keep hypocrisy at bay is for us to realize its root cause. In the above passage in Luke, Jesus mentions "fear" or "afraid" five times. He is teaching us that *the basic cause of hypocrisy is the fear of men.*

When we are afraid of what others may say about us or do to us, we pretend we are something else to gain their approval. The scribes and Pharisees in Jesus' day were more concerned about reputation than character. They were more focused on what people thought about them than what God knew about them.

As Proverbs 29:25 states, *"The fear of man brings a snare."* Jesus desires that we avoid such a trap.

A minister named Dr. F. E. Marsh told about the time he was preaching on the importance of confession of sin and, wherever possible, of making restitution for wrong done to others. After the sermon, a young man came up to him and said: "Pastor, you have put me in a sad fix. I have wronged another and am ashamed to confess it. I have talked to this person often about his need of Christ and have urged him to come and hear you preach, but he scoffs and ridicules it all."

The young man continued, "In my work, copper nails are used because they do not rust in the water. But they are quite expensive, so I had been carrying home quantities of them to use on a boat I am building in my back yard."

The pastor's sermon had brought him face to face with the fact that he was just a common thief. "But," he said, "I cannot go to my boss and tell him what I have done, or offer to pay for those I have used. If I do he will think I am just a hypocrite, and yet those copper nails are digging into my conscience, and I know I will never have peace until I put this matter right."

Some time later he came again to Dr. Marsh and exclaimed, "Pastor, I've settled the copper nails issue, and my conscience is relieved at last."

"What happened when you confessed?" asked the pastor.

"Oh, he looked at me a little funny and then said, 'George, I always thought you were just a hypocrite, but now I begin to feel there's something in this Christianity after all. Any religion that makes a dishonest workman confess that he has been stealing copper nails, and offer to settle for them, must be worth having.'"

It's time to shine the light in the dark places and vacuum the dust! Jesus says the remedy for hypocrisy is to forget what people may say, think, or do, and fear God alone!

This cures all our anxieties, because he who fears God fears nothing else. The worst man can do is kill the body; after that he can do no more. Only God can condemn the soul to Hell—He is the final judge. But remember, our heavenly Father cares for us more than He cares for the sparrows. We are of greater value to Him, so we need not fear man.

Legalism says God will love us if we change. The Gospel says God will change us because He loves us.

– TULLIAN TCHIVIDJIAN

Chapter 4

The Yoke Breaker

People are often unreasonable and self-centered. Forgive them anyway. If you are kind, people may accuse you of ulterior motives. Be kind anyway. If you are honest, people may cheat you. Be honest anyway. If you find happiness, people may be jealous. Be happy anyway. The good you do today may be forgotten tomorrow. Do good anyway. Give the world the best you have and it may never be enough. Give your best anyway. For you see, in the end, it is between you and God. It was never between you and them anyway.

– Mother Teresa

As we talk about the yoke of Jesus, we need to remember it does speak forgiveness to the individual, but it does not excuse or approve of sin. It is not about compromising the integrity of the Word of God to overlook iniquity. We cannot escape the fact that the world is lost without Christ and it is our mission to tell the Good News of the Gospel to every individual He places in our path. Those who receive the message will have forgiveness and hope, but those who reject it will experience eternal separation from God.

> *As for you, you were dead in your transgressions and sins, in which you used to live when you followed the ways of this world and of the ruler of the kingdom of the air, the spirit who is now at work in those who are disobedient. All of us also lived among them at one time, gratifying the cravings of our flesh and following its desires and thoughts.*
>
> *Like the rest, we were by nature deserving of wrath. But because of his great love for us, God, who is rich in*

mercy, made us alive with Christ even when we were dead in transgressions—it is by grace you have been saved. And God raised us up with Christ and seated us with him in the heavenly realms in Christ Jesus, in order that in the coming ages he might show the incomparable riches of his grace, expressed in his kindness to us in Christ Jesus.

For it is by grace you have been saved, through faith—and this is not from yourselves, it is the gift of God—not by works, so that no one can boast. For we are God's handiwork, created in Christ Jesus to do good works, which God prepared in advance for us to do (Ephesians 2:1-10 NIV).

I love to be an answer to someone's prayer, don't you? To be able to get in on an unusual miracle is one of the joys of my life.

Recently I left a marriage conference on a cold Sunday night. Heading home I noticed my gas tank was getting close to empty, so I decided to stop and fill up. Normally I just pull up to the pump, use my card, and never go inside the station. It was such a chilly night, and I knew that it would take more than the fifty dollar limit to fill up my tank. Since, I didn't want to stand in the brisk air, I decided to go inside to pay.

As I was standing at the counter ready to pay for a couple of sodas, I didn't want to eavesdrop, but I could not help overhearing this attractive young woman standing next to me talking to the clerk about her situation. She was explaining that she was pregnant and her boyfriend wanted her to get an abortion. Everyone, including her boyfriend had abandoned her.

I could sense from the sound of her voice that she was totally stressed and confused about what to do. This was her first child and all she kept saying was, "I don't know what to do. And I don't know how I'm going to make it." She was wearing the heavy yoke of shame.

After the young woman finished explaining her situation, I looked at her and asked her name. Then I said, "Do you mind if I pray for you?"

She glanced at me for a moment with a startled expression and I quickly explained who I was and that I felt the Lord wanted me to pray for her and the baby. Finally she agreed, "Sure."

I began to pray, and I declared that this child was a gift from God. I prayed a blessing over her and let her know in no uncertain terms that there are no accidents with God. As tears welled up in her eyes, I reassured her that she had not been abandoned by God. Others may turn their back, but I wanted her to know that the Lord would walk by her side every step of the way! It was my joy to introduce this troubled young woman to the "Yoke Breaker!"

After I finished praying I reached in my pocket and handed her some money. She quickly said, "Oh, I can't accept that." All I knew to say was that it was God's money and He wanted her to have it.

I went on to explain that the Lord brought me, a preacher, into this store at this appointed time to let her know that her future was secure. God was in total control and her unborn child had a destiny, because the Lord doesn't make mistakes.

It was as if a revival broke out at the market! She walked out of the store with a smile on her face, rejoicing and shouting "Hallelujah"—with hope for tomorrow. She later visited our church and testified to God's goodness.

You may think the Lord has forgotten you, but remember, He is never late and always on time. That is the amazing yoke of Jesus!

JESUS IS THE YOKE BREAKER!

Isaiah looked through the corridors of time and prophesied there would come a day when the Anointed One would be on the scene. He would break off the yoke of oppression, heaviness, and the unbearable weight of religion.

Although the primary application of the following verses applies to the bondage of the Assyrians, the message is real for our time. *"It shall come to pass in that day that his burden will be taken away from your shoulder, and his yoke from your neck, and the yoke will be destroyed because of the anointing oil"* (Isaiah 10:27).

"When that time comes, I will free you from the power of Assyria, and their yoke will no longer be a burden on your shoulders" (Isaiah 10:27 GNT).

The yoke is figurative of bondage and affliction. *"I am the Lord your God, who brought you out of the land of Egypt, that you should not be their slaves; I have broken the bands of your yoke and made you walk upright"* (Leviticus 26:13).

What kind of yoke has religion placed on you?

- Jealousy?
- Fear?
- Bitterness?
- Hurt?
- Depression?
- Pride?
- Envy?
- Unforgiveness?
- Shame?

"'For it shall come to pass in that day,' says the Lord of hosts, 'that I will break his yoke from your neck, and will burst your bonds; foreigners shall no more enslave them'" (Jeremiah 30:8).

The Yoke Breaker is Now on the Scene

> *As Jesus was walking beside the Sea of Galilee, he saw two brothers, Simon called Peter and his brother Andrew. They were casting a net into the lake, for they were fishermen. "Come, follow me," Jesus said, "and I will send you out to fish for people."*
>
> *At once they left their nets and followed him. Going on from there, he saw two other brothers, James son of Zebedee and his brother John. They were in a boat with their father Zebedee, preparing their nets. Jesus called them, and immediately they left the boat and their father and followed him* (Matthew 4:18-22 NIV).

The first disciples called by God's Son were professional

fisherman. Then, to the shock of everyone, He called a tax collector. *"As he walked along, he saw Levi son of Alphaeus sitting at the tax collector's booth. 'Follow me,' Jesus told him, and Levi got up and followed him"* (Mark 2:14 NIV). In the culture of the day, a tax collector was considered wealthy.

A TIME FOR TESTING

To follow Jesus always brings tests. Someone said, "You never fail one of His tests; you just get to take it over again until you pass." I don't know about you, but I like to pass an exam the first time around. When you read the ministry of Jesus, it seems that at every turn, the disciples were taking another test. For example:

- He gave them a *provision* test. In John 6 He said, "How are we going to buy enough food to feed this crowd?"
- He gave them a *trust* test. In Mark 4 He said, "Let us cross over to the other side." He knew full well a storm was brewing.
- He gave them a *timing* test. In John 11 He wanted to see how they would react when He delayed concerning their good friend Lazarus, who was sick and eventually died.
- He gave them a *loyalty* test. In Matthew 26 and John 19 they were all tested. When arrested, tried, convicted, and crucified, would they stand by His side?

I would love to say that they passed each exam the first time, but that would not be true. Remember, these men were disqualified by their religion. They were not graduates of rabbinical school. They did not have the advantage of education, but that did not stop Jesus from putting them on the fast track of discipleship. He was more interested in their future than their past. The number one attribute the rabbis were looking for when calling disciples was, "Do they have the necessary passion and drive to surpass the works that I do as their teacher?"

Jesus said, *"Very truly I tell you, whoever believes in me will do the works I have been doing, and they will do even greater things than these, because I am going to the Father"* (John 14:12 NIV).

It was obvious that He believed in them more than they believed in themselves.

The Tests Start Early

When Jesus called His first disciples, they were immediately sent to the classroom to take their first exam—and the tests never seem to let up. The list is too long to enumerate here, but suffice it to say that Jesus was getting them ready to change the world. In order for them to accomplish the mission, they had to pass the test and graduate.

We don't know the conversation that took place between James, John, Simon Peter, and Andrew when Jesus talked to them. Using my sanctified imagination I can see Jesus pointing to Matthew the tax collector (IRS agent) and saying to the other disciples, "If you're going to follow My yoke, can you forgive this man who has been stealing from you?"

It was not unusual in that culture for tax collectors to line their own pockets with excess taxes. No doubt they knew Matthew, and understood what he was all about.

Jesus was teaching them the first component of His yoke. He was letting them know, "You are not the disciple of Judaism or any of the rabbis. Their yoke teaches condemnation and judgment. My yoke teaches to love and forgive."

The demonstration of following Rabbi Jesus is clearly outlined in Scripture: *"A new command I give you: Love one another. As I have loved you, so you must love one another. By this everyone will know that you are my disciples, if you love one another"* (John 13:34-35 NIV). *"My command is this: Love each other as I have loved you"* (John 15:12 NIV).

We will never be identified as a disciple of Rabbi Jesus if we harbor unforgiveness, bitterness, prejudice, resentment, and hatred in our hearts. It is not possible. If you and I are to be disciples of Christ, we do not have the authority or "Semicha" to form our own interpretation of His yoke or teaching. The only thing we can do is fulfill His yoke. It is to be repeated and imitated, not reinterpreted.

Many problems have infected the body of Christ because we take His teachings and restate them through the lens and the filter of our own prejudices?

For example, on the subject of holiness, there are many different viewpoints. Author Christopher Momany writes in *Ministry Matters*:

> *What is Christian holiness? For many, holiness is a kind of goodness they can never reach. For others, it is a religious doctrine once taught and now forgotten. For most, it is perhaps an intimidating or even irrelevant notion Holiness is living in relationship with God, not using minor rules against others.*
>
> *However, holiness is not living without regard for God's law or intended way of life for us. However, most would affirm that holiness is nothing without love. Therefore a careful consideration of love confronts every seeker after holiness, and this consideration must be grounded in the biblical witness and informed by principled theological reflection.*

Some people define holiness by what they don't do. Holiness is not a set of rules and regulations—the wearing of jewelry, the cutting of the hair, a certain dress code, or reading from a specific version of the Bible. And, that's just a short list. I'm sure you could add more.

I live in the South; some would call it the Bible Belt. It is a known fact that in many Southern churches you will be condemned to hell for drinking a glass of wine, or smoking a cigarette, but it's perfectly acceptable to hold hate for other races. You will be condemned for going to movies, or cutting your lawn on Sunday afternoon, but it's quite alright to gossip about other church members.

We layer our yoke on top of the yoke of Jesus and justify our own interpretation of what He taught. Preachers have been known to stand in the pulpit and condemn the congregation for going to sporting events, or even worse: going out to eat at a restaurant that serves mixed drinks. Yet, they find nothing wrong with being two hundred pounds overweight and needing help to walk up to the podium!

There's something wrong with this picture! We want mercy for ourselves and justice for everyone else. This may be a shock to your system, but God is in the forgiveness business and does not hold our past sins or excesses against us. He does not have an "enemies" list.

J. C. Ryle, the Bishop of Liverpool, England, in the nineteenth century, was right: "We must be holy, because this is one grand end and purpose for which Christ came into the world. Jesus is a complete Savior. He does not merely take away the guilt of a believer's sin, He does more—He breaks its power (1 Peter 1:2; Romans 8:29; Ephesians 1:4; 2 Timothy 1:9; Hebrews 12:10). My fear is that as we rightly celebrate, and in some quarters rediscover, all that Christ saved us from, we will give little thought and make little effort concerning all that Christ saved us to."

The yoke of our Rabbi is merciful. As it is written, *"For judgment is without mercy to the one who has shown no mercy. Mercy triumphs over judgment"* (James 2:13).

The Bible and human history is filled with men and women who would be disqualified from speaking in many, if not most churches today because of past failures.

People of every generation have been exposed to horrible mistakes. Even at the beginning, Adam and Eve endured failure. They had a perfect environment filled with everything their hearts could desire. God called them to make the earth beautiful and fill it with children to enjoy.

It all changed when Satan moved into this utopia and began tempting Adam and Eve with the idea that they could be as wise as God. "Just eat this, and you will know what you're missing." You've read the rest of the story.

There were many others named in the Bible who failed in some way or another. I'm not only talking about the "bad" or the insignificants, but God's champions. Yes, even the chosen and commissioned ones experienced failure. I'm sure they never dreamed their errors and mistakes would be recorded and still talked about thousands of years later.

For example:

- Abraham's wife, Sarah, who convinced him to have a child by another woman.
- Samson, the strongest man who ever lived, could not control his wild nature, leading to his downfall at the hands of a woman.
- King David, a courageous warrior, creative musician, and man after the very heart of God, fell victim to uncontrolled desires leading to adultery and murder.
- Solomon, perhaps the wisest man in the Old Testament, eventually neglected his time with God and lost the intimacy that he once knew. At the end of his life he was a bitter and lonely man.
- Elijah, who possessed enough courage to issue a challenge to 450 prophets of Baal, was brave enough to confront King Ahab, but the threat of one woman caused him to run for his life. His depression was so great that he wanted to die.
- Saul, later Paul, was considered a murderer by his own admission. He was complicit in the death of Stephen and tried to destroy the early church.

Although the Bible records the downfall of many, it also details how these champions rose from the pit of defeat to conquer the enemy called failure.

Would you hire this man?

Let me share this story by an unknown author:

A church was in need of a pastor for some time but was having trouble getting one; but not because pastors weren't applying, but because the congregation always seemed to find fault with the pastors. Most pastors were rejected after their resumes were read. Some didn't have enough experience, some too much, some not enough education, some too much and so on.

One day a board member, who was getting very

tired of this, decided to do something. So the next Sunday, he stood up in the pulpit and announced that he had another résumé to share with the congregation. Most of them sat back, folded their arms and began to listen, ready to see what faults they could find on the new applicant. The board member began to read and the résumé went like this...

"Dear church members; I am writing to apply for position as your pastor. My experience is more along the lines of evangelist but I believe I could fill your position adequately. I've never attended any bible school per say but I have a lot of field experience. I don't have a degree on my wall, or a wall for that matter; I've traveled around most of my life, renting and doing odd jobs to support myself and preaching wherever I was invited; churches, streets, even jails. As a matter of fact, I've been thrown in jail several times and been involved in a few public squabbles. I've been accused of being anti-semitic, anti-authority and causing disturbances almost everywhere I go. But I did have a few conversions to Christianity during my ministry as well as a few healings. Thank you for considering my application."

Most of the people looked up at the deacon with smirks of condemnation while others chuckled out loud. One man stood up and still laughing asked the deacon, "Does this guy actually expect us to seriously consider him for our pastor? Just what's this fellow's name any way?"

The deacon replied that the letter was signed—the Apostle Paul! You could have heard a pin drop.

As you can see, Paul would not have been a "fit" for most congregations. Would you hire a man with his background? Not in *today's* church!

Cheer up. All is not lost. The yoke of Rabbi Jesus is being demonstrated in many places all over the world. A pastor friend of mine tells the following true story:

I was sitting in my office one Tuesday afternoon when my secretary buzzed me on the intercom and said there was a man wanting to see me. She said, "Pastor, be careful. He looks rough and very troubled."

As Jim (not his real name) sat down, I asked him "What can I do to help you?" He said, "Preacher, I can't sleep, I can't eat, my conscience is killing me. I have done some things that I am ashamed of and I don't know what to do about it."

After a little more discussion I discovered that Jim was nothing more than a common thief. He made his living robbing houses while people were at work. After telling me everything he wanted to say, I looked at him and said, "Jim do you know Jesus?" He answered, "No, I am not a Christian, but something has to change!"

I took my Bible, spent a considerable amount of time, and led him to faith in Christ. After we finished praying, Jim looked at me with tears in his eyes and said, "Preacher, I need to tell you something else." I held my breath and replied, "Go ahead and get it all out of your system." He pointed to the pickup truck sitting out on the street and told me, "I just robbed a house this morning and all of the stuff is still in my truck. What should I do now?"

I said, "Well Jim, I would love to be able to tell you to just return the stuff and get on with your life, but it doesn't work that way. My advice is to go to the owner of the home, throw yourself on his mercy and see what happens. If he decides to call the police and have you arrested you have to pay the price."

Jim announced, "As soon as I leave here, I'm going to do just that."

The next day I was coming in from lunch and I saw Jim driving his old beat-up pickup truck into the church parking lot. I was rather surprised. I thought he might call me from the county jail. Instead he came by to tell me what happened. "Preacher, I went back to the home that I robbed and confessed to the owner what I had done. He told me to replace all of the items and he would not call the police. Jim said the owner told him that he was a Christian and believed in forgiveness. He told me he had past failures in his own life and yet God had forgiven him."

I called Bob (the homeowner) and asked him if all of this was true. He confirmed what had happened and then he said something that astounded me. "Pastor are you going to baptize Jim anytime soon?" I replied. "Yes, we're going to baptize him this Sunday night."

Bob asked, "Do you mind if I come and worship with you and watch Jim being baptized?" I answered ,"Of course not. You are welcome. As a matter of fact, why don't you help me baptize him?" There was a long pause on the other end of the line, then finally Bob said, "It would be my joy. I would be honored."

The next Sunday night Jim, myself, and Bob, the man who was robbed, stood in the baptismal pool and listened as Jim confessed to the entire congregation the transformation that had taken place in his life. He pointed to Bob and said with tears streaming down his face and a quiver in his voice, "If this is a demonstration of real Christianity, this is what I've been looking for my whole life!" The congregation erupted in "Hallelujah! Hallelujah!" as Bob and I had the privilege of baptizing Jim!

THE YOKE BREAKER IS PUT TO HIS OWN TEST

The Gospel of John is a window into the constant confrontation between the yoke of Jesus and the yoke of religion.

- He was confronted with regard to the Sabbath (John 5:1-18).
- He was confronted with regard to His Sonship (John 5: 19-29).
- He was confronted with regard to the Scriptures (John 5:30-47).
- He was confronted by life's shortages (John 6:1-15).

- He was confronted by life's storms (John 6:16-21).
- He was confronted by seekers (John 6:22-71).

One of the most pointed confrontations takes place in John 8:2-11. The Pharisees and scribes were constantly trying to find ways to trap Jesus and thus nullify His yoke.

> *At dawn he appeared again in the temple courts, where all the people gathered around him, and he sat down to teach them. The teachers of the law and the Pharisees brought in a woman caught in adultery. They made her stand before the group and said to Jesus, "Teacher, this woman was caught in the act of adultery. In the Law Moses commanded us to stone such women. Now what do you say?" They were using this question as a trap, in order to have a basis for accusing him.*
>
> *But Jesus bent down and started to write on the ground with his finger. When they kept on questioning him, he straightened up and said to them, "Let any one of you who is without sin be the first to throw a stone at her."*
>
> *Again he stooped down and wrote on the ground. At this, those who heard began to go away one at a time, the older ones first, until only Jesus was left, with the woman still standing there. Jesus straightened up and asked her, "Woman, where are they? Has no one condemned you?" "No one, sir," she said. "Then neither do I condemn you," Jesus declared. "Go now and leave your life of sin"* (John 8:2-11 NIV).

The very heart of the yoke of Jesus is forgiveness. Here, He is called to judge a woman taken in the very act of adultery. The Pharisees needed judgment from a rabbi with Semicha. Make no mistake, she was not coming to Jesus to repent. She was brought before Him because she got caught. The situation He was faced with was not pushed on Him unexpectedly, nor was He surprised. The question of guilt was a foregone conclusion.

It's interesting to see two contrasting sins. One is the woman dragged before him in the nakedness of her adultery, and two, the scribes and Pharisees in the horror of their self-righteousness.

Here are the players in this dramatic encounter:

- Rabbi Jesus.
- The Jerusalem committee on morality (The scribes and Pharisees).
- A woman caught in the act of adultery.
- Students who were being taught by Rabbi Jesus at the temple.
- The curious crowd who was always on the fringe to watch the show.

There are three issues at stake: (1) What to do with the woman taken in adultery, (2) what would Jesus do with the self-righteous leaders? and (3) how to handle the trap set for Jesus.

The Pharisees pressed, *"'Teacher, this woman was caught in the act of adultery. In the Law Moses commanded us to stone such women. Now what do you say?' They were using this question as a trap, in order to have a basis for accusing him"* (John 8:4-6).

The ambush was set. On one hand, if Jesus said "Stone her," they would say that He lacked compassion and mercy. The very heart of His teaching (His yoke) would be compromised. If He answered, "Let her go," they would have accused Him of breaking the Law of Moses. They knew Jesus associated with the worst of the worst. He hung around with the disqualified, the very ones who were told they would never be good enough to make it into heaven. They also knew all too well that Jesus insisted in His teaching, *"I come not to call the righteous but sinners to repentance."* It looked like they had a perfect plan. But perfect plans don't always work out!

Picture the Scene:

The door burst open with a loud crack. The committee on purity and morality was staging a raid. Cold, unforgiving hands yanked the woman out of bed screaming in her ear, "Get up, you have been caught, it's time for your judgment, you tramp!"

She could feel the heat of their vitriolic scorn—"You have

shamed yourself and your family. You are disgusting and pathetic." They probably didn't give her enough time to properly cover herself before they marched her through the city so everyone would know about her sin. As if it weren't enough to be caught in the act, now all of Jerusalem became judge and jury and rendered its verdict: guilty as charged!

To add insult to her shame, the men threw her in the middle of a morning teaching being led by Jesus at the temple. As the stunned students looked on, her pious accusers began to question Jesus concerning His yoke. The Jerusalem morality police set the trap. The law says to stone her, what does Your yoke say?

The woman had no place to hide. She couldn't deny the accusation; she had been caught. Beg for mercy? From whom? No point in asking God, because His representatives were standing there with their stones in hand and snarling their lips ready to crush her with judgment. If she was hoping for compassion, there was none to be found here, or so she thought.

You must remember, among the Jews, adultery was considered the worst possible sin a person could commit. Adultery is the sin of fornication committed by someone who is married. The marriage bond was broken and, in the mind and heart of the culture, she could not have done anything more horrific. But at no point did Jesus condone her sin, or approve her actions.

Marriage is a beautiful picture of the relationship between Christ and the believer. To commit adultery is a slap in the face of Jesus, as if to say, "I don't want any part of living in a union with Jesus Christ."

You will find in the Old Testament the prophets explaining to Israel that their relationship to God was a marriage relationship. Hosea, Ezekiel, and others pointed to this bond. I believe the woman knew that. She knew her life was destroyed and she would be considered the worst possible sinner. Imagine if you will, being caught in the very act and dragged before Jesus.

No one would speak for her, but someone would *stoop* for her. Jesus does an unusual thing. Verse 6 says, *"Jesus stooped down and wrote in the dust."*

Quite frankly, I would have expected Jesus to stand squarely in the face of the religious yoke and speak, but instead He leaned over and began to write in the sand. He descended lower than anyone else—beneath the moral policeman, the people, even beneath the accused woman. The pious ones looked down their noses on her. To see Jesus, they had to look down even farther.

Jesus was prone to stoop:

- He stooped to wash the feet of His disciples.
- To embrace children.
- He stooped to pull Peter out of the sea.
- To pray in the garden at His darkest hour.
- He stooped before the Roman whipping post.
- He stooped to carry the cross.

Grace is a God who stoops!

Here, He bent down to write in the sand. For centuries there has been speculation as to exactly what Jesus wrote. One of the best explanations I have read came from Bible teacher and professor Herman Hanko:

> *The Bible doesn't explain to us why He stooped down. The Bible doesn't tell us what He wrote on the ground. So perhaps it's better if we just keep silent about it and say nothing at all. Why then does the Holy Spirit tell us that He stooped down not once but twice to write on the ground? It's almost as if the Holy Spirit who calls us to witness this event says to us, 'Notice this.' Where in the Bible is something like this referred to which will perhaps help us to understand the strange conduct of Jesus?*
>
> *The answer to that is, surprisingly enough, in the prophecy of Jeremiah:"O Lord, the hope of Israel, all that forsake You shall be ashamed. 'Those who depart from Me shall be written in the earth, because they have forsaken the Lord, the fountain of living waters'" (Jeremiah 17:13).*
>
> *It could be that the first time Jesus stooped to write He was writing the Scripture. The scribes and Pharisees may have thought, "He is just trying to get out of it, trying to avoid the issue." They grew impatient with the stooping Jesus and demanded an answer. So He stood up not to*

teach, His words were very few, and not for long, He would soon stoop again for a second time."

The answer they received was not what they expected. Their perfect plan was being blown up by the Yoke Breaker. Jesus told them, "All right, stone her. That's what the law says, so go ahead. But, before you do, My yoke says, 'Let those who have never sinned throw the first stone!'"

He was literally saying, "Those who have never committed the "same sin" cast the first stone. Rabbi Jesus put His yoke (interpretation) on top of traditional teaching: *"You have heard that it was said, 'You shall not commit adultery.' But I tell you that anyone who looks at a woman lustfully has already committed adultery with her in his heart"* (Matthew 5:27-28 NIV).

Then He stooped down again and wrote in the dust. The sound of rocks falling to the ground must have been deafening. Name-callers shut their mouths. Jesus resumed His scribbling. When they heard what He said, they all left, one by one, the older men first.

Jesus was now alone with the woman standing there. He straightened up and asked, "Where are they? Is there no one left to condemn you?" "No one, sir," she answered. "Well, then," Jesus replied, "I do not condemn you either. Go, but do not sin again."

The witnesses were gone. The law says only by two witnesses can you be stoned. They all left! Jesus couldn't make the act of her sin go away, so He made her accusers go away. According to the law a mistrial must be declared!

"Where are your accusers?" That is a question, not just for the woman, but for you and me. We all have heard the voices of condemnation. Who is it that continually charges us with failure? Who screams in your ear?

- "You will never be good enough."
- "You have failed—again."
- "You will never improve, because you're stupid."
- "Stop trying. God is finished with you."
- "You messed up before, and you will do it again."

Who is this cop standing on the corner of our mind that never shuts up? The apostle John tells us: *" The great dragon was hurled down—that ancient serpent called the devil, or Satan, who leads the whole world astray. He was hurled to the earth, and his angels with him. Then I heard a loud voice in heaven say: 'Now have come the salvation and the power and the kingdom of our God, and the authority of his Messiah. For the accuser of our brothers and sisters, who accuses them before our God day and night'"* Revelation 12:9–10 (NIV).

What does an accuser do? He accuses. The Holy Spirit brings conviction that leads to repentance, but the accuser's condemnation brings no repentance, just regret. The mission of the accuser is to *"steal, and to kill, and to destroy"* (John 10:10).

Satan will rob you of your dreams, kill your peace, and destroy your hope for the future. He will use anyone to bring guilt and condemnation. He has his own travel agency for guilt trips. He has no shame; he will recruit friends, church members, parents and even coworkers. It doesn't matter to him as long as the mission is accomplished.

BUT—SATAN WILL NOT HAVE THE LAST WORD!

As Max Lucado has so beautifully written:

> *Jesus has acted on your behalf. He stooped. Low enough to sleep in a manger, work in a carpentry shop, sleep in a fishing boat. Low enough to rub shoulders with crooks and lepers. Low enough to be spat upon, slapped, nailed, and speared. Low. Low enough to be buried.*
>
> *And then he stood. Up from the slab of death. Upright in Joseph's tomb and right in Satan's face. Tall. High. He stood up for the woman and silenced her accusers, and he does the same for you. He stands up. He "is in the presence of God at this very moment sticking up for us"* (Romans 8:34 MSG).
>
> *Let this sink in for a moment. In the presence of God,*

in defiance of Satan, Jesus Christ rises to your defense. He takes on the role of a priest. "Since we have a great priest over God's house, let us come near to God with a sincere heart and a sure faith, because we have been made free from a guilty conscience" (Hebrews 10:21-22, NCV).

A clean conscience. A clean record. A clean heart. Free from accusation. Free from condemnation. Not just for our past mistakes but also for our future ones. "Since he will live forever, he will always be there to remind God that he has paid for [our] sins with his blood" (Hebrews 7:25 TLB). Christ offers unending intercession on your behalf.

Satan is left speechless and without ammunition. But fortunately, you and I have an advocate with the Father (1 John 1:21). We do not have to listen to the accuser's voice, because it takes two witnesses to condemn according to the law. When Satan stands to accuse us before the throne of God, our Defense Attorney, Jesus, holds up nail pierced hands and shows the blood contract and declares, "Justified, not guilty!"

The accusations fall on deaf ears because God is the one who justifies based on the sacrifice of His very Son. When God looks at you and me, He doesn't see our sin; He sees us covered in the blood. Remember, the next time the voices of condemnation speak about your past, your Defense Attorney is speaking on your behalf, declaring*, "There is therefore now no condemnation to those who are in Christ Jesus."* (Romans 8:1).

The message to the woman caught in adultery and to us is this: the Yoke Breaker is here. The love of God always wins the day. So, the next time Satan brings up your past, bring up his future! Or, just tell him, "Be quiet. I'll see you in court. You can take it up with my Defense Attorney, Rabbi Jesus. He's never lost a case!"

Chapter 5

Warning! Beware of the Grace Killers

I have found, in my own spiritual life that the more rules I lay down for myself, the more sins I commit. The habit of regular morning and evening prayer is one which is indispensable to a believer's life, but the prescribing of the length of prayer, and the constrained remembrance of so many persons and subjects, may gender unto bondage, and strangle prayer rather than assist it.

– Charles Spurgeon

In these first chapters we have established the fact Jesus was not an ordinary Rabbi. Jesus was a Rabbi with Semicha. According to Hebrew tradition, for a rabbi to have Semicha (authority to interpret Scripture) he had to be recognized as a prophet from God, himself, or, as Aaron and Moses had traditionally given authority to 70 elders, they had to be certified as having Semicha by two other rabbis with the same designation.

When Jesus was challenged about His authority, He would simply remind them of what happened at His baptism. He pointed them to John, the dove, and the voice from heaven that resounded throughout Israel. They had no answer for this because there were too many witnesses to the events.

Jesus explained, "I only do what the Father tells Me to do and I only say what the Father tells Me to say." He didn't answer to the high priest, but to His heavenly Father—and for that they hated

Him even more. They knew He was no ordinary rabbi; He was one with Semicha, and fulfilled all requirements necessary. *"Come to me, all you who are weary and burdened, and I will give you rest. Take my yoke upon you and learn from me, for I am gentle and humble in heart, and you will find rest for your souls. For my yoke is easy and my burden is light"* (Matthew 11:28-30 NIV).

Remember, when Jesus spoke those words, He was contrasting His yoke with the yoke of legalism exemplified and embodied in the teachings of the rabbis. The essence of rabbinic instruction was seen in the attitude and actions of the scribes, Pharisees, and Sadducees. They were "guardians" of the law. It is a fact they added to the law to make sure everyone understood what God really meant, as if they were God's voice.

They considered themselves the final authority on all matters of religious tradition. We look back on this group of men and see how harsh Jesus dealt with them (See Matthew 23). However, in the cultural context, they were considered the fulfillment of all righteousness by the common people. In other words, they were seen as "super saints." The average Jew was being controlled and intimidated by these so-called pious ones.

Legalism did not die when Jesus rose from the dead. On the contrary, like tiny specks of leaven, it infiltrated the early church. As it spread, the leaven of legalism was ever present. Constant battles were fought on many different fronts to combat rules and regulations in the church.

The yoke (their interpretation of Scripture) of legalism is quick to assume the worst and disqualify anyone who does not meet their standards of holiness. However, the yoke of Jesus is quick to forgive and easy to carry. Jesus emphasizes love and forgiveness which triumphs the handbook of the legalist.

In his book, *Fan the Flame,* author Joseph Stowell writes:

> *In contrast to the two commands of Christ, the Pharisees had developed a system of 613 laws, 365 negative commands and 248 positive laws. By the time*

Christ came it had produced a heartless, cold, and arrogant brand of righteousness. As such, it contained at least ten tragic flaws:

1. *New laws continually need to be invented for new situations.*
2. *Accountability to God is replaced by accountability to men.*
3. *It reduces a person's ability to personally discern.*
4. *It creates a judgmental spirit.*
5. *The Pharisees confused personal preferences with divine law.*
6. *It produces inconsistencies.*
7. *It created a false standard of righteousness.*
8. *It became a burden to the Jews.*
9. *It was strictly external.*
10. *It was rejected by Christ.*

I believe it would be fair to say that legalism has not changed much in the last 2,000 years. It was alive and well during the ministry of Jesus and the formation and spread of the early church. Through the centuries it has reared its ugly head and can be seen in the 21st century church. Some would say, "Legalism—the same yesterday, today, and forever."

WHAT IS LEGALISM?

Legalism is the human attempt to gain salvation or prove our spirituality by outward conformity to a list of religious do's and don'ts. The sad truth is that legalism is often disguised as spirituality, obedience, or maturity. It is not wrong to have personal standards and convictions in your life, but it is wrong to judge another's Christianity, spirituality, or maturity by your convictions or personal prejudices.

Here's how Bible scholar, Daniel Taylor, expresses this in his book, *The Myth of Certainty*:

> *The great weapon of authoritarianism, secular or religious, is legalism: the manufacturing and manipulation of rules for the purpose of illegitimate control. Perhaps the most damaging of all the perversions of God's will and Christ's work, legalism clings to law at the expense of grace, to the letter in place of the spirit.*
>
> *Legalism is one more expression of human compulsion for security. If we can vigorously enforce an exhaustive list of do's and don'ts (with an emphasis on external behavior), we not only can control unpredictable human beings but have God's favor as well.*
>
> *Legalistic authoritarianism shows itself in the confusion of the Christian principle of unity with a human insistence on unanimity. Unity is a profound, even mystical quality. It takes great effort to achieve, yet mere effort will never produce it; it is a source of great security, yet demands great risk.*
>
> *Unanimity, on the other hand, is very tidy. It can be measured, monitored, and enforced. It is largely external, whereas unity is essentially internal. Its primary goal is corrected behavior, while unity's is a right spirit. Unanimity insists on many orthodoxies in addition to those of belief and behavior, including orthodoxy of experience and vocabulary. That is, believers are expected to come to God in similar ways, to have similar experiences with God, and to use excepted phrases in describing those experiences.*

FREEDOM ALWAYS COMES WITH A PRICE

In 1775, freedom was on the lips and in the hearts of the colonists. On March 23 of that year, Patrick Henry, a passionate and determined 39-year-old attorney, stood before the convention of the Virginia Commonwealth and declared:

> *If we wish to be free we must fight! I repeated it, sir, we must fight! An appeal to arms, and to the God of hosts, is all that is left us. It is vain, sir, to extenuate the matter. The gentleman may cry "Peace, peace!" But there is no peace. The war has already begun! Our brethren are already in the field. Why stand we here idle? Is life so dear or peace so sweet as to be purchased at the price of chains and slavery? Forbid it, Almighty God. I know not what course others may take, but as for me, give me liberty or give me death!*

Because of the courage and boldness of Patrick Henry. a young nation was stirred to action. His name will forever be associated with freedom.

THE MEANING OF BEING FREE

What does freedom really mean? Rabbi Jesus made a profound statement on the topic:

> *To the Jews who had believed him, Jesus said, "If you hold to my teaching, you are really my disciples. Then you will know the truth, and the truth will set you free."*
>
> *They answered him, "We are Abraham's descendants and have never been slaves of anyone. How can you say that we shall be set free?" Jesus replied, "Very truly I tell you, everyone who sins is a slave to sin. Now a slave has no permanent place in the family, but a son belongs to it forever. So if the Son sets you free, you will be free indeed."* (John 8:30–36 NIV).

It is obvious that the people Jesus was addressing were confused about freedom. It's hard to imagine a first century Jew saying, "We have never been in bondage to any man!" All you have to do is read Old Testament history and see what a ridiculous statement that was.

The Jewish nation was often in bondage because of God's discipline. The cycle would repeat itself over and over again. Disobedience would lead to discipline. God would send foreign nations to exercise His judgment. When Israel could not stand before their enemies, they realized repentance was the key that would lead to deliverance. When you read the book of Judges you will see a perfect example of the cycle.

Centuries later, at the moment Jesus was speaking these words, the nation of Israel was under the iron boot of the Roman government.

Everyone desires freedom, but to enjoy it you must grasp the yoke of Jesus in three distinct principles:

1. God's original design for man is freedom.

Many interpret freedom as "no rules, no boundaries, and no restraint." However, such an attitude often leads to rebellion at best and anarchy at worst.

Suppose the people of your city decided they wanted freedom from traffic laws? No more stop signs, no more red lights, and no more rules about driving too fast. How long do you think it would take for your city to dissolve into chaos? Freedom is not the elimination of rules and restraint, nor is it doing whatever you feel like.

Peter Marshall, a former chaplain of the United States Senate, prayed this prayer before the elected officials, "Lord Jesus, thou who art the way, the truth, and the life; hear us as we pray for the truth that shall make all free. Teach us that liberty is not only to be loved but also to be lived. Liberty is too precious a thing to be buried in books. It costs too much to be hoarded. Help us see that our liberty is not the right to do as we please, but the opportunity to please to do what is right."

Freedom is the privilege that we share with Christ, who gives us the power to become all that God designed us to be. It is the great opportunity to see our potential fulfilled to the glory of Christ.

Are you living to your full potential?

Let's look at the *Oxford Dictionary* definitions of potential: (1) having or showing the capacity to develop into something in the future; (2) latent qualities or abilities that may be developed and lead to future success or usefulness; (3) the possibility of something happening or of someone doing something in the future.

You cannot always act in a manner which is inconsistent with the way you see yourself. It is a sad thing to know that the majority will never discover who they really are, while others settle for only a portion of their true potential. We all have the same ability to make the decision to fully use the gifts, talents, abilities, and capabilities that have been placed within us. The question is, will we exercise the option to maximize our potential?

Dr. Myles Munroe describes potential this way, "Potential, the unexposed, untapped, hidden, dormant revelations that lay beneath the accumulated dust and grime of many years. Potential. Strength and beauty that lay unmarred by the ravages of fire, wind, and water. The possibilities of rebuilding after years of destruction, decay, and neglect."

When you pick up your Bible you are opening a book of freedom. From Exodus to Revelation the emphasis is on liberty.

Real freedom begins with the new birth, but remember, Jesus said, *"Whoever commits sin is the servant of sin"* (John 8:34). Literally translated He is referring to whoever is in the habit of practicing sin.

If you and I continually disobey God, that's not freedom, but bondage. The new birth in Christ sets you free from condemnation, and the gives you the power to overcome sin. Why give up your freedom for moments of pleasure that will only result in shame and guilt?

2. God has a method to keep us free.

The power of the Almighty works through truth. It's the exact opposite of Satan, who operates through lies. Jesus called Satan a liar and the father of lies (See John 8:44).

While God uses truth to bring you into freedom, the devil uses deceit to wrap you in the chains of bondage. His first lie was perpetrated in the Garden of Eden. After God warned that if Adam and Eve ate from the tree of the Knowledge of Good and Evil, they would die, Satan said, *"You will not surely die"* (Genesis 3:4).

Then the devil made this astounding promise to them, *"...you will be like God"* (verse 5). Satan was offering them three things:

1. Freedom without responsibility.
2. Freedom from consequences.
3. Freedom without eternal judgment.

People today are still believing the same lie that man can do as he wishes because in the final analysis he is his own God. Paul expressed deep concern for those who *"worshiped and served the creature rather than the Creator"* (Romans 1:25).

In the river of God's truth, which is His method for freedom, there are three distinct currents.

First, Jesus is the truth (John 14:6). When you have a personal relationship with Christ, you know God's living truth, which sets you free.

Second, the Word of God is truth (John 17:17). When we spend time meditating and studying the Scriptures, we have truth.

Third, the Holy Spirit is truth (1 John 5:6). *"When He, the Spirit of truth, has come, He will guide you into all truth"* (John 16:13). And *"Where the Spirit of the Lord is, there is liberty"* (2 Corinthians 3:17).

3. Jesus Christ is God's revelation of truth.

Because God's Son experienced freedom Himself, He can

promise freedom to all those who believe in Him. *"So if the Son sets you free, you will be free indeed"* (John 8:36).

Christ came to a nation that was not only under bondage from Rome, but was under the yoke of religious and political subjection. The yoke of religion disqualified and condemned, but Jesus refused to bow down to the traditions of men. The more you know Jesus the more freedom you experience and enjoy. Here's how the Apostle Paul expressed it: *"I want to know Christ—yes, to know the power of his resurrection and participation in his sufferings, becoming like him in his death"* (Philippians 3:10 NIV).

The amazing thing is this: the more you become like the Lord Jesus, more opportunities for releasing your potential will be available. Freedom is a life controlled by truth and motivated by love.

HEED THE WARNING! THERE ARE GRACE KILLERS AT WORK!

The issue of legalism continues to rear its ugly head. As Bible scholar S. Louis Johnson wrote in *Theological Quarterly*:

> *One of the most serious problems facing the Orthodox Christian church today is the problem of legalism. One of the most serious problems facing the church in Paul's day was the problem of legalism. In every day it is the same. Legalism wrenches the joy of the Lord from the Christian believer, and with the joy of the Lord goes his power for vital worship and vibrant service. Nothing is left but cramped, sober, dull, and listless profession. The truth is betrayed, and the glorious name of the Lord becomes a synonym for a gloomy killjoy. The Christian under law is a miserable parody of the real thing.*

We must be on guard because there are Grace Killers waiting to rob us of our freedom in Christ. After the resurrection and ascension of Jesus, when the first disciples began to spread the

Good News, it seemed only natural to them to share their message with Jewish people. Their early ministry was concentrated in Jerusalem. Later, after Stephen's death, as they were scattered and began to spread out across the near east, they continued to preach almost exclusively in the synagogues. They used the Old Testament to show Jesus was the promised Messiah, and their overriding concern was for their fellow Jews to accept the Gospel.

Then strange things began to happen. Some believers had the peculiar idea of taking the message of Jesus and sharing it with non-Jews, with people like us, Gentiles. Not only that, but it seemed that God was actually blessing their work. Many Gentiles were becoming followers of Jesus.

Even Peter seemed to be caught up in this unusual phenomenon, with apparently some strange vision of unclean animals and a visit to, of all people, a Roman centurion. As soon as the Gospel was received by the Gentiles (See Acts 10-11), legalism rose up again. It was difficult, if not impossible for those who were Pharisees converted to Christianity to wrap their minds around the grace of God. They did everything possible to mix legalism (circumcision, and keeping the Law of Moses) with faith in Christ. Their attitude was that in order to be an acceptable Christian you must do both. They felt that salvation must be maintained by keeping the Law of Moses and a person was not really saved if they didn't keep the Ten Commandments.

Immediately after the Holy Spirit fell on the house of Cornelius, Peter was questioned about his experience. All he could do was recount his vision on the rooftop and the instructions given to him by the Holy Spirit to go with men to this particular house and preach the gospel of grace. After hearing Peter's explanation, *"they had no further objections and praised God, saying, 'So then, even to Gentiles God has granted repentance that leads to life'"* (Acts 11:18 NIV). End of discussion; case closed.

The Gentiles received the Gospel by faith, nothing else required, right? Wrong! There was a storm brewing, and it exploded in Acts 15.

After all, if you were a Gentile, you weren't circumcised. You weren't educated in the Old Testament and in the Law of Moses. You could have grown up worshiping some other god and had a background in a pagan cult. How on earth could you possibly be included within God's chosen people? What right did you have to be considered a genuine follower of Jesus?

It is little wonder that Acts 15 begins with some men traveling from Judea (the Roman province that included Israel—to Antioch—where many Gentiles had become Christians) and saying that unless you are circumcised, according to the custom taught by Moses, you cannot be saved.

PAUL, BARNABAS, AND PETER TAKE A STAND

Certain people came down from Judea to Antioch and were teaching the believers: "Unless you are circumcised, according to the custom taught by Moses, you cannot be saved." This brought Paul and Barnabas into sharp dispute and debate with them.

So Paul and Barnabas were appointed, along with some other believers, to go up to Jerusalem to see the apostles and elders about this question. The church sent them on their way, and as they traveled through Phoenicia and Samaria, they told how the Gentiles had been converted. This news made all the believers very glad. When they came to Jerusalem, they were welcomed by the church and the apostles and elders, to whom they reported everything God had done through them. Then some of the believers who belonged to the party of the Pharisees stood up and said, "The Gentiles must be circumcised and required to keep the Law of Moses."

The apostles and elders met to consider this question. After much discussion, Peter got up and addressed them: "Brothers, you know that some time ago God made a choice among you that the Gentiles might hear from my lips the message of the gospel and believe. God, who

> *knows the heart, showed that he accepted them by giving the Holy Spirit to them, just as he did to us. He did not discriminate between us and them, for he purified their hearts by faith.*
>
> *Now then, why do you try to test God by putting on the necks of Gentiles a yoke that neither we nor our ancestors have been able to bear? No! We believe it is through the grace of our Lord Jesus that we are saved, just as they are* (Acts 15:1-11 NIV).

Had it not been for the vigorous defense of the gospel of grace by these men, we might be living a different kind of Christian life today. Grace was hanging in the balance and the grace killers were met on the battlefield of God's truth—and were defeated.

Again, Peter is defining legalism as a yoke. The very yoke that confronted Jesus during His earthly ministry is now threatening the spread of the Gospel. In no uncertain terms, Peter tells the council that since no one had been able to bear this yoke over the centuries, why were they testing God?

After much discussion and heated debate, James rendered his decision: *"It is my judgment, therefore, that we should not make it difficult for the Gentiles who are turning to God. Instead we should write to them, telling them to abstain from food polluted by idols, from sexual immorality, from the meat of strangled animals and from blood"* (Acts 15:19-20 NIV).

Again, you would think the question was settled once and for all. Wrong! The spirit of legalism walked away from the Jerusalem Council meeting and said, "You may have won this battle, but the war is not over, you will hear from us again!" Nowhere are the grace killers more exposed than Paul's declaration in his letter to the Galatians. *"It is for freedom that Christ has set us free. Stand firm, then, and do not let yourselves be burdened again by a yoke of slavery"* (Galatians 5:1 NIV).

The Judaizers (legalists) declared, "The doctrine of grace that Paul preaches is dangerous! He must be stopped at all cost. He is replacing the Law with license. If we have no rules or set standards of behavior, the churches will fall apart."

The Judaizers in Paul's day are not the only ones who are afraid to depend on the liberty and freedom of God's grace. Our churches are filled with legalists who warn people about the liberty they enjoy in Christ. They claim liberty leads to religious anarchy and a license to sin. Nothing could be farther from the truth. The believer who lives by faith experiences the internal discipline of the Holy Spirit which is far better than man-made rules and regulations.

To live with the higher law of love and grace is not the dangerous yoke. It is legalism that is a danger, because it attempts to do in the flesh what can only be accomplished through the Holy Spirit.

The yoke of Jesus says:

- You have been set free. You are no longer under bondage to the law (Galatians 5:1-12).
- You need someone to control your life from within not from without. That someone is the Holy Spirit (Galatians 5:13-26).
- My love abides in you, and you now have the desire to live for others and not for yourself (Galatians 6:1-10).

The yoke of legalism says:

- I will become more spiritual if I obey the rules.
- I have the willpower to obey all rules and regulations to improve myself.
- Since I don't do some of the things I used to do, I must be better than others in my church.
- God is certainly blessed to have me. If only others were like me, the church would be a better place.
- How wonderful it is to be so spiritual; it's too bad that others are not as spiritual as I am.

It's no wonder that Paul considered legalism an insidious and dangerous enemy. Any way you look at it, when you walk away from grace in favor of the law, you always lose! Paul put on his armor and probably said, "Let's get ready to rumble!" (My interpretation).

Paul, the freedom fighter, tries to explain to these Galatian believers what they lose by exchanging grace for law.

1. Hello slavery. Goodbye freedom.

Paul describes the law as a yoke: *"Do not be entangled again with a yoke of bondage"* (Galatians 5:1). Where have we heard that before? Yes, it's the same thing that Peter said in Acts 15, so Here we go again.

Why does Paul compare the law to a yoke? Yokes are used with animals. The law, like a yoke is used to control us. The truth is, the law never changes anybody; and in spite of the fact that we do have laws, some still live like animals. But what would the world be like if there were no laws? God revealed His righteousness in the law. It was used to warn man, but in spite of the warning, man still chose to rebel against the Almighty.

According to Galatians, Jesus Christ bore the curse of the law when He died on the cross (Galatians 3:13). When you and I became Christians we exchanged the external yoke of legalism for the internal yoke of love. I remind you that the Savior said, *"Come to me, all you who are weary and burdened, and I will give you rest. Take my yoke upon you and learn from me, for I am gentle and humble in heart, and you will find rest for your souls. For my yoke is easy and my burden is light"* (Matthew 11:28-30 NIV).

The yoke of the law brought restlessness and agony, but the yoke of Jesus brings rest to our souls. In spite of all of this, Paul had to deal with this issue with the churches of Galatia. They were in danger of exchanging their freedom for bondage. He reminds them that when they trusted Jesus, they lost the yoke of slavery to sin and put on the yoke of Christ. Instead of living under a hard, heavy weight, Jesus proclaimed that His yoke is easy and His burden is light.

2. You now have a debt you cannot pay.

> *Stand fast therefore in the liberty by which Christ has made us free, and do not be entangled again with a yoke of bondage. Indeed I, Paul, say to you that if you become circumcised, Christ will profit you nothing. And I testify again to every man who becomes circumcised that he is a debtor to keep the whole law. You have become estranged from Christ, you who attempt to be justified by law; you have fallen from grace. For we through the Spirit eagerly wait for the hope of righteousness by faith. For in Christ Jesus neither circumcision nor uncircumcision avails anything, but faith working through love* (Galatians 5:1-6).
>
> *Having canceled the charge of our legal indebtedness, which stood against us and condemned us; he has taken it away, nailing it to the cross. And having disarmed the powers and authorities, he made a public spectacle of them, triumphing over them by the cross* (Colossians 2:14-15 NIV).

If you have ever owed money, you know something about the stress of indebtedness. Paul was saying the law was against us, and trying to keep the law was not freedom, but a debt we could not pay. The law was never given to save people, it was given to show men and women they needed to be saved. It was against us because it exposed sin and revealed the holy and righteous judgments of God. We cannot obey it no matter how hard we try.

In Galatians 5, Paul reminds the believers of their debt by using three phrases:

- "Christ will profit you nothing" (verse 2).
- "A debtor to...the whole law" (verse 3).
- "You have become estranged from Christ" (verse 4).

Paul draws a sad conclusion, "You have fallen from grace." He is not talking about losing salvation. Rather, it means when you try to mix grace and law you are moving out of the sphere of God's grace. Nine times he calls them "brethren," and his letter deals with them as believers in Christ. If he were saying they were lost he would never say, *"Because you are his sons, God sent the Spirit of his Son into our hearts, the Spirit who calls out, 'Abba, Father.'"* (Galatians 4:6 NIV).

By moving toward another gospel they robbed themselves of the riches that are found in the grace of God. When you live by grace you depend on the power of the Spirit, but to move back under the law you depend on your own efforts and abilities to make yourself approved before God. All of the attempts of man combined can never produce what faith can accomplish through the work of Jesus on our behalf.

3. Like a runner who gets off course—you lose your direction.

> *You were running a good race. Who cut in on you to keep you from obeying the truth? That kind of persuasion does not come from the one who calls you. "A little yeast works through the whole batch of dough." I am confident in the Lord that you will take no other view. The one who is throwing you into confusion, whoever that may be, will have to pay the penalty.*
>
> *Brothers and sisters, if I am still preaching circumcision, why am I still being persecuted? In that case the offense of the cross has been abolished. As for those agitators, I wish they would go the whole way and emasculate themselves!* (Galatians 5: 7-12 NIV).

On more than one occasion Paul used athletic illustrations to highlight a spiritual truth. He knew the Olympic Games (which began in 776 BC) always included foot races. While he never uses the image of a race to tell people how to receive Christ, Paul talks to believers about how to live the Christian life.

A literal reading of verse 7 says, "You are running well. Who cut in on you so that you stopped obeying the truth?" It was mandatory for the competitors to stay in their assigned lane, but it's also true that some would cut in on their competition to try to knock them off course. This is exactly what happened to the Galatian believers. The Judaizers cut in on the gospel of grace preached by Paul and forced them to take a detour.

From the beginning of his letter to the end, Paul has one central theme. Watch out for the grace killers; like yeast (verse 9), it only takes a small bit, but left alone it grows and permeates the whole. The Judaizers were planting small bits of leaven, and if the believers were not vigilant, it would grow and eventually destroy them.

IT'S TIME TO EXPOSE THE METHODS OF THE GRACE KILLERS

How do they worm their way in? Two devious ways:

First: By teaching a perverted gospel (Galatians 1:6-10).

Paul did not beat around the bush. He says it plain and simple; legalists twist the truth and somehow convince others to let Moses finish what Christ started. It's a salvation by human achievement, which is a perversion of the gospel of grace. Legalism says, "Work hard, sacrifice as much as possible, give your money, and attend as many meetings as possible. Your good works will cause God to approve of you." God's grace says, "You have nothing to give, nothing to earn, and nothing to pay. Salvation is a gift and it cannot be bought. God is too rich to sell and you are too poor to buy!"

The reason for Paul's teaching was needed *"because some false believers had infiltrated our ranks to spy on the freedom we have in Christ Jesus and to make us slaves. We did not give in to them for a moment, so that the truth of the gospel might be preserved for you"* (Galatians 2:4-5 NIV).

Paul refused to give in to their legalistic demands.

Liberty has always been worth fighting for. For example, in 1852, Wendell Phillips stood before a meeting of the Massachusetts anti-slavery coalition and declared, *"Eternal vigilance is the price of liberty!"*

That statement is valid today, not only in the realm of the political, but even more so in the realm of the spiritual.

The legalists came in as spies. A. T. Robertson defines the phrase, "to spy out" as, "to reconnoiter, to make a treacherous investigation."

What was the purpose of spying on their liberty? Only one reason I can think of. It is to enslave! The goal of the legalists is to always make others endure the same bondage in which they live. Paul, the freedom fighter, wanted to make sure they got the message.

Eugene H. Peterson, in his inspiring book, *Traveling Light,* observes:

> *There are people who do not want us to be free. They don't want us to be free before God, accepted as we are by his grace. They don't want us to be free to express our faith originally and creatively in the world. They want to control us; they want to use us for their own purposes.*
>
> *They themselves refuse to live arduously and openly in faith, but huddle together with a few others and try to get a sense of approval by insisting that we all look alike, talk alike and act alike, and thus validating one another's worth. They tried to enlarge their numbers only on the condition that new members act and talk and behave the way they do. These people infiltrate communities of faith "to spy out our freedom which we have in Christ Jesus" and not infrequently find ways to control, restrict and reduce the lives of free Christians.*
>
> *Without being aware of it, we become anxious about what others will say about us, obsessively concerned about what others think we should do. We no longer live the good news but anxiously tried to memorize and recite the*

script that someone else has assigned to us. In such an event we may be secure, but we will not be free.

But Paul, "did not yield in submission even for a moment, that the truth of the gospel might be preserved for you." Every free person who benefits from Paul's courage will continue vigilance in the resistance movement he formed.

Second: They practice hypocrisy (Galatians 2:11-14).

It is always a shock and surprise to see who can be influenced by legalism. Paul recounts a dramatic confrontation between himself and Peter. Why would Paul rebuke Peter? It is not a mystery.

One informal translation of verse 23 says, *"He was in the habit of eating his meals with the Gentiles. That went on until the Jews showed up. And when they did... 'Oh, no thanks, I never eat ham,' lied Peter, hoping to make the Jews smile in approval. The problem was that before James and his Jewish friends arrive, ol' Peter could be heard saying to his Gentile cronies, 'Sure, serve it up. Add a little bacon while you're at it. I love the taste!' Hypocrite!"*

Paul rebuked Peter publicly to expose his hypocrisy. Peter was called on the carpet for his duplicity. He was saying one thing to the Gentiles, and turning around and acting differently in front of his Jewish friends. Where I come from that is speaking out of both sides of your mouth!

On one hand, Peter was talking freedom (with the smell of ham on his breath), and on the other hand he was talking law (with the smell of hypocrisy on his life), and the fact is he was not living either one. Paul said, "Peter make up your mind get on one side of the fence or the other!"

This reminds me of the story of a rather pompous-looking deacon who was endeavoring to impress upon a class of boys the importance of living the Christian life. "Why do people call me a Christian?" the man asked. After a moment's pause, one youngster said, "Maybe it's because they don't know you."

HYPOCRISY WILL ALWAYS PRODUCE COLLATERAL DAMAGE

Peter's duplicity had an impact on others. The Bible records that *"the rest of the Jews also played the hypocrite with him, so that even Barnabas was carried away with their hypocrisy"* (Galatians 2:13).

Barnabas, a close friend of Paul and an encouragement to many, was even duped into believing Peter was right. Barnabas had been one of the spiritual leaders of the church in Antioch (See Acts 15), so his disobedience would have influence on many others. I'm convinced if their hypocrisy had won the day, the church at Antioch would have become nothing more than a Christian sect. It would have died a slow, painful death with a mix of Judaism and Christianity.

Grace Killers Cannot be Ignored or Tolerated.

Legalism, once recognized, cannot be allowed to exist—not any more than allowing a black widow spider to slip into your bed, and you do nothing about it. Eventually somebody is going to be bitten! Since our freedom in Christ is worth fighting for, what can you do?

1. Stand firm in your freedom and do not give in.

Continually ask God for courage when faced with the Grace Killers. As author Elmer Davis wrote, "This will remain the land of the free only so long as it is the home of the brave." This also applies to the church.

2. Refuse to curry favor with others.

If your circle of friends intimidate and manipulate you, it's time to find a new circle of friends. Never allow yourself to be controlled by others simply because you want their favor and approval.

3. Don't be afraid to speak the truth in love.

When faced with error, it is never right to be mean-spirited;

rather, speak the truth in love. In the mind and heart of Paul, his freedom in Christ was worth far more than popularity or even security. He was willing to fight for that liberty.

I like what Warren Wiersbe said in his book, *Be Free*:

> *Modern day Judaizers, like their ancient counterparts, reject the authority of Paul and try to undermine the gospel which he preached. In Paul's day, their message was "the gospel plus Moses."*
>
> *In our day it is "the gospel plus" any number of religious leaders, religious books, or religious organizations. "You cannot be saved unless..." It is their message and that "unless" usually includes joining their group and obeying their rules. If you dare to mention the gospel of grace is preached by Jesus, Paul, and the other apostles, they reply, "But God has given us a new Revelation!"*

Paul has an answer for them: *"If any man preach any other gospel unto you that you have received, let him be accursed!"* (Galatians 1:9).

Grace, grace. God's grace. It's the message of freedom.

Chapter 6

Running on Empty

Don't burn out; keep yourselves fueled and aflame. Be alert servants of the Master, cheerfully expectant. Don't quit in hard times; pray all the harder. Help needy Christians; be inventive in hospitality. Bless your enemies; no cursing under your breath. Laugh with your happy friends when they're happy; share tears when they're down. Get along with each other; don't be stuck-up. Make friends with nobodies; don't be the great somebody. Don't hit back; discover beauty in everyone.

– Romans 12:11-17 MSG

We have already learned that Jesus was the only rabbi in Israel with Semicha, or the authority to interpret Scripture. The body of teaching for a rabbi with Semicha was called his yoke. When questioned about this, Jesus made it very clear He did not come to destroy the law, but to fulfill it. He put His template of interpretation on top of the existing law and lifted it to a higher level.

This gives us more insight as to why Jesus drew such large crowds. It was not because He would feed them, but because He was offering them a better way of life. His yoke was polar opposite from what had been taught them since childhood. The unqualified, helpless, and downtrodden flocked to hear Him. Not because He would work miracles, but because they had been longing for a fresh word from heaven. Like lighting a candle in a dark room, the words of Jesus illuminated their hearts and allowed them to see there was hope for the hopeless. For the first time they were hearing it was possible to have a personal relationship with Yahweh.

The religious authorities were not against Him because He drew crowds. Their complaint was that Jesus was perverting the established teachings of the rabbis and destroying the traditions of the elders. He spoke of loving your enemies, while they spoke of an eye for an eye. He taught to forgive, they taught condemnation.

The actions of the religious system was a perfect example of the "means justify the ends." It made no difference to them who they hurt or what they did, the only thing that mattered was that this rabbi called Jesus had to be stopped.

ARE YOU SICK AND TIRED OF BEING SICK AND TIRED?

The yoke of Christ is best encapsulated in Matthew 11:28-30: *"Come to me, all you who are weary and burdened, and I will give you rest. Take my yoke upon you and learn from me, for I am gentle and humble in heart, and you will find rest for your souls. For my yoke is easy and my burden is light"* (Matthew 11:28-30 NIV).

Now I want you to see the same Scripture from The Message translation: *"Are you tired? Worn out? Burned out on religion? Come to me. Get away with me and you'll recover your life. I'll show you how to take a real rest. Walk with me and work with me—watch how I do it. Learn the unforced rhythms of grace. I won't lay anything heavy or ill-fitting on you. Keep company with me and you'll learn to live freely and lightly."*

The questions Christ asked were not just for that day, but for you and me. Many are living on the treadmill of life; running as fast as they can and getting nowhere. Life has become boring and mundane, one day bleeding into another.

The reason reading Matthew 11 brings peace and rest to our souls is because so many people are living under a heavy yoke of bondage. Men and women are desperate to find a way to ease their troubled minds that robs their rest, steals their joy, and leaves them without the assurance that God is in control.

When you live under a heavy yoke, you become a slave and

not the master. Remember, *"It is for freedom that Christ has set us free. Stand firm, then, and do not let yourselves be burdened again by a yoke of slavery"* (Galatians 5:1 NIV).

This may be:

- The yoke of denominational pressure.
- The yoke of traditionalism.
- The yoke to live and act a certain way, contrary to how you see yourself.
- The yoke of the Devil's lies.
- The yoke of the deadly trifecta—family, friends, and finances.
- The yoke of insecurity.
- The yoke of weariness.

If you are exhausted and worn out, it's not because of the yoke of Jesus. As we have already seen He is the "yoke breaker," not the "yoke maker." Whatever you are facing that is causing stress, upset, and even ulcers is not coming from the One who created you and loves you without measure. God's original design was for the fulfillment of your purpose, which brings freedom, not a life filled with heaviness, anxiety, and depression.

The Dutch-born Christian author, Henri J. M. Nouwen, wrote, "Try to give your agenda to God. Keep saying, 'Your will be done, not mine.' Give every part of your heart and your time to God and let God tell you what to do, where to go, when and how to respond. God does not want you to destroy yourself. Exhaustion, burnout, and depression are not signs that you are doing God's will. God is gentle and loving. God desires to give you a deep sense of safety in God's love. Once you have allowed yourself to experience that love fully, you will be better able to discern who you are being sent to in God's name."

There is one club that has millions of members. It carries different names, but I saw a description that you may find easy to recognize. If approached to join, run far away. It's called the "Coronary and Ulcer Club." If you are a member, quit. To be a card-carrying member there are certain rules:

1. Your job comes first. Forget everything else.
2. Saturdays, Sundays, and holidays are fine times to be working at the office. There will be nobody else there to bother you.
3. Always have your briefcase with you when not at your desk. This provides an opportunity to review completely all the troubles and worries of the day.
4. Never say "no" to a request. Always say "yes."
5. Accept all invitations to meetings, banquets, committees, etc.
6. All forms of recreation are a waste of time.
7. Never delegate responsibility to others. Carry the entire load yourself.
8. If your work calls for traveling, work all day and travel at night to keep that appointment you made for eight the next morning.
9. No matter how many jobs you are already doing, remember you can always take on more.

The Anatomy of Burnout

According to Ken Crockett, in *The 911 Handbook,* "Burnout occurs when we give out more than we take in. We go from giving out to giving up. Cars that aren't refueled will run out of gas. Wells that are not replenished will run dry. Batteries that are not recharged will have no power. We are not any different. A Christian that is not refueled, replenished, and recharged will burn out."

Are You Suffering from This Ailment?

- Does Gospel preaching leave you empty?
- Do you put your mind in neutral during praise and worship?
- Does watching your favorite sports team get you more excited than being a follower of Jesus?
- Do you find yourself being more critical of church services than you used to be?

- Do those smiling, happy-clappy Christians make you nervous?
- Are you afraid that someone will ask you what you have learned from your personal devotions?

If so, you may be suffering from a common spiritual disease we've been talking about called—burnout. This may cause you to envision a variety of images, such as the fire-charred shell of a house or building. However this is not limited to physical objects. Burnout happens in every walk of life; to business executives, classroom teachers, marriage partners, students, preachers, and children of God.

No one is immune, especially those of us who are in some form of ministry. Burnout is something we know about but never discuss. Why? If we admit to this condition, we are afraid of being accused of not being spiritual, so it's best to keep our mouths shut. Many Christians find it's much easier to "fake it" because we have learned the language of passion, even if its fire is burning low.

ELIJAH IS A CLASSIC OLD TESTAMENT EXAMPLE OF BURNOUT

There have been many spiritual giants who suffered from weariness and fatigue, but none more pronounced and exposed than the prophet Elijah.

In 1 Kings 19:4 we learn of Elijah's exhaustion: *"But he himself went a day's journey into the wilderness, and came and sat down under a broom tree. And he prayed that he might die, and said, "It is enough! Now, Lord, take my life, for I am no better than my fathers."*

Why was he so depressed? Had he committed some crime? No. He had simply declared the truth. He did what was right, and what he received in return were death threats from the Queen of Israel. This hurt him deeply. Like Elijah, nearly all of us experience times when our spiritual fires diminish or when God seems distant.

What lessons can we learn from Elijah's experience?

1. Running on empty will lead to burnout.

The great prophet's desert depression was preceded by the Mount Carmel triumph. Elijah had been on the mountain three days earlier, engaged in a remarkable confrontation with the pagan priests of Baal. This was the age of Ahab and Jezebel in which God judged the land with a "no rain" edict for three years. Elijah had challenged the priests to a duel of sorts, and by the end of the day he had scored a spectacular victory

Talk about passion! One man against a spiritually depraved nation and a powerful king and queen. God answered his prayer with force! A simple prayer, an explosion of fire, and the God of Elijah was vindicated (1 Kings18:36-38).

The next thing Elijah knew he was running for cover. He had received death threats from Queen Jezebel who was upset at the humiliating defeat of her god at Mount Carmel. Elijah was so afraid that *"he arose and ran for his life, and went to Beersheba, which belongs to Judah, and left his servant there"* (verse 3).

He could have said, "The God who was with me on the mountain will be with me in the valley. I didn't run from the false prophets and I won't run from this wicked Queen."

Instead, he made a desperate plea to God: *"But he himself went a day's journey into the wilderness, and came and sat down under a broom tree. And he prayed that he might die, and said, 'It is enough! Now, Lord, take my life, for I am no better than my fathers!'"* (verse 4).

It's hard to believe that this was the same man who stood strong and faced down evil. Now he was running on empty. Elijah was depressed, ready to lie down and give up. But instead of allowing him to die, God gave him exactly what he needed. Elijah was in dire need of food, rest, and sleep.

When the gas gauge on your car says empty, you know it's time to fill up. If you feel burned out it could be because of over-work, over-commitment, and trying to be a super-hero to everyone. Even the Lord Jesus needed time to be alone and refresh Himself.

It Happened in New York

One of the most tragic events in aviation happened on January 25, 1990. Avianca Flight 52 from Colombia crashed just 15 miles short of New York's Kennedy International Airport, killing 73 passengers. The reason: the plane just ran out of gas.

Under international regulations, an airliner must carry enough fuel to reach its destination as well as its assigned alternate, plus extra to handle at least 45 minutes of delays. Due to low fuel, the Avianca pilots had requested "priority" (not "emergency") landing. Because the exact word "emergency" was not used, and due to heavy traffic and bad weather conditions, the ill-fated plane was placed on a holding pattern—until it simply ran out of gas.

2. Unfulfilled expectations will lead to burnout.

"And let us not grow weary while doing good, for in due season we shall reap if we do not lose heart" (Galatians 6:9).

Burnout can take place when we feel nothing is happening. We receive a clear vision, and a word from God, yet time goes by and our vision remains unfulfilled. What we see around us does not mesh with what we feel on the inside.

It's always a good idea to stop and ask the Lord, "Give me heaven's perspective on this situation." While we are looking at time, God is looking at timing. There is no vision that is is going to unfold in an instant. While it's true that God promises success, He never said it was easy or would be accomplished in a single day.

3. Unconfessed sin will lead to burnout.

Although Elijah's discouragement was not caused by his disobedience, sin remains the number one reason for spiritual burnout. Sin buried beneath the surface will do great harm. Just as cancer starts with a rebellious cell and spreads to the rest of the body if unchecked, so is unconfessed sin.

David knew this to be true. He said in Psalm 139:23-24 NIV: *"Search me, God, and know my heart; test me and know my anxious thoughts. See if there is any offensive way in me, and lead me in the way everlasting."*

Ask yourself:

- Am I engaged in anything that would dull my spiritual passion?
- Am I harboring any offenses or unforgiveness toward anything or anyone?
- Am I holding onto something that will douse my spiritual flame?

If so, you will undoubtedly become a casualty of spiritual burnout.

4. Majoring on the externals of religion to the neglect of a personal relationship will produce burnout.

The yoke of religion is steeped in repetitious formality. Remember, Jesus was going counter to one of the strongest religious systems known to man. The rules, regulations, and traditions used to control people became nothing more than a heavy burden no one could bear.

As Scottish minister George MacDonald observed, "Nothing is so deadening to the divine as a habitual dealing with the outsides of holy things."

Jesus hit the issue head on: *"You hypocrites! Isaiah was right when he prophesied about you: "These people honor me with their lips, but their hearts are far from me. They worship me in vain; their teachings are merely human rules"* (Matthew 15:7-9 NIV).

All of us would agree a relationship with your spouse should never become ritualistic or a habit. Neither should a relationship with Jesus. We attend church to worship, not to have our ticket punched for the week. Prayer is essential and a two-way conversation, not something we do because it's expected. Discipline is good, but if we're not careful it will lead us into the dangerous waters of ritualism, and not a personal relationship with Christ.

KEYS TO LIGHTING THE FIRE AGAIN

If you are dealing with spiritual burnout, all is not lost. God told Elijah to do four things to get out of the pit. If you follow the same advice, there is hope.

First: Take time to rest.

The last thing Elijah needed was a lecture and scolding from God. The Almighty didn't say, "You just need to get it together. What's wrong with you; don't you know that you can whip yourself into shape? Do I need to remind you that just two days ago you were the big man on campus?—and now look at you, hiding under a broom tree!"

No, God didn't yell at him, because He knew exactly what Elijah needed. His first remedy was rest, sleep, and food. I love Psalm 127:2 in the Living Bible: *"God wants his loved ones to get their proper rest."*

Sometimes the most spiritual thing you can do is go to sleep. Vince Lombardi, the famous coach of the Green Bay Packers, once said, "Fatigue makes cowards of all of us."

2. Let it out—God can take it.

Have you ever been around a person who blew up at the slightest comment? You walk away feeling like you've just been hit with a blast from a double-barreled shotgun.

You think, "All I said was, 'How are you today?' And the next thing I knew a volcano of emotions erupted."

It may be that you just encountered someone with the the Elijah syndrome. People everywhere are suffering from spiritual Post-Traumatic Stress Disorder (PTSD). A soldier exposed to constant combat without rest, sleep, proper nutrition, and a time to vent, is in danger of this condition. Likewise, a believer exposed to stress, pressure, and unfulfilled expectations is also at risk.

It's only when we get to the point that we can be honest with ourselves and God that healing will ever occur. Usually the things that are out of control in our lives are what we refuse to verbally express. If you can't talk about it, you probably can't manage it.

Elijah had enough! The volcano erupted!

And the word of the Lord came to him: "What are you doing here, Elijah?" He replied, "I have been very zealous for the Lord God Almighty. The Israelites have rejected your covenant, torn down your altars, and put your prophets to death with the sword. I am the only one left, and now they are trying to kill me too."

The Lord said, "Go out and stand on the mountain in the presence of the Lord, for the Lord is about to pass by."

Then a great and powerful wind tore the mountains apart and shattered the rocks before the Lord, but the Lord was not in the wind. After the wind there was an earthquake, but the Lord was not in the earthquake. After the earthquake came a fire, but the Lord was not in the fire. And after the fire came a gentle whisper.

When Elijah heard it, he pulled his cloak over his face and went out and stood at the mouth of the cave. Then a voice said to him, "What are you doing here, Elijah?" He replied, "I have been very zealous for the Lord God Almighty. The Israelites have rejected your covenant, torn down your altars, and put your prophets to death with the sword. I am the only one left, and now they are trying to kill me too."

The Lord said to him, "Go back the way you came, and go to the Desert of Damascus. When you get there, anoint Hazael king over Aram. Also, anoint Jehu son of Nimshi king over Israel, and anoint Elisha son of Shaphat from Abel Meholah to succeed you as prophet. Jehu will put to death any who escape the sword of Hazael, and Elisha will put to death any who escape the sword of Jehu. Yet I reserve seven thousand in Israel—all whose knees have not bowed down to Baal and whose mouths have not kissed him (1 Kings 19:9-18 NIV).

What's a nice prophet like you doing in a place like this?

"What are you doing here, Elijah?" He replied, "I've been very zealous for the Lord, but..." Underline that word, "but."

Here's my interpretation of Elijah's response: "God, I've done everything You have asked me to do. When You told me to go and pronounce your judgment to King Ahab, I walked straight in and told him what You said without fear. They could have killed me, but I didn't care because I was following Your plan for my life. Let's face it God, I'm all You have left!"

The Lord wasn't shocked with Elijah's griping or with the way he felt. When the prophet expressed, "God, I'm angry, bitter, depressed, and lonely," the Lord wasn't surprised. God didn't say, "You shouldn't feel that way." He listened.

The Creator knows your feelings better than you do. After all, He wired you! He just wants you to understand your emotions, and by talking them out it helps you get in touch with what you're feeling and thinking. God promises, "I'll listen as long as you want to talk, until you run out of words."

There is no emotion you could reveal to the Lord that would make Him stop loving you or cause Him to become upset.

He says, "If you want to get well, first you rest your body, then release your frustrations, your emotions."

So if you are feeling stressed out, uptight, and overloaded, do what the Bible says: "*Humble yourselves, therefore, under God's mighty hand, that he may lift you up in due time. Cast all your anxiety on him because he cares for you*" (1 Peter 5:6-7 NIV).

Once you come to the place where you know it's all right to pour out your heart to Jesus, and tell Him honestly how you feel, you will be amazed at how quickly the heaviness will dissipate. Remember, God never meant for you to carry that heavy load.

3. Redirect your focus.

God is about to give Elijah another key to overcome his burnout. The prophet is to witness a massive demonstration of the Lord's power. God has a purpose, and it's not to show Elijah that He can put on a spectacular pyrotechnic event for him.

The Creator gave an awesome display of earth, wind, and fire (1 Kings 19:11-12) to remind Elijah of one central fact: "I am God, and you're not! Name your problem, Elijah. My power is greater than anything you might face. If you will just focus on Me, you will be amazed at how small your problems become."

One of the fastest ways to burn out is to believe that we have to control everything. It's not that we think we are God, it's just that we act like we can handle every situation we face.

I am reminded of what David said in Psalm 100:3 NIV: *"Know that the Lord is God. It is he who made us, and we are his; we are his people, the sheep of his pasture."*

In this verse, David makes it very clear that we are not God! This may be a shock to your system, but he actually calls us sheep. To be considered sheep may sound warm and fuzzy, but I'm not sure it was a compliment. In fact, sheep are:

- Dumb
- Defenseless
- Directionless

The root of all burnout is playing God. You and I were created by Him and for Him. We need to wake up and realize that the Lord never intended for us to manage every detail of our lives. Super-heroes are fun to watch in the movies, but God did not wire us to be Superman and Superwoman.

A quick cure for burnout is to make God bigger than your problems. If you are feeling stressed to the max, allow God's grace to overwhelm and strengthen you. Don't allow yourself to live by what others say about you. Instead, wrap your mind around the Lord's unconditional love and watch what happens.

4. Get back in the game.

I can always tell when I'm around someone struggling with burnout. All they want to talk about is themselves. It only takes one to have a pity party.

No matter what difficulties you're going through, you can always find an individual whose problems are bigger than yours. A fast way out of the pit of burnout is to find a person to help.

Try applying the Luke 6:38 principle: *"Give, and it will be given to you. A good measure, pressed down, shaken together and running over, will be poured into your lap. For with the measure you use, it will be measured to you"* (NIV).

This verse is not just talking about material things. If you need to feel encouraged, be an encouragement to someone else. If you need a friend, be a friend. If you think no one cares, then find a person to care about. The principal works. The more you give the more you receive.

In 1 Kings 19:15-18, God puts Elijah back to work. When the prophet declared that he was the only one serving, God reminds him that He has others Elijah doesn't even know about. He said, "Elijah, it's time to get out of the pit, it's not over. Go and find these men. Join with them and get on with your assignment."

Centuries later, when Jesus came to earth, He declared, "By giving your life away, you will find it."

Elijah needed to get his eyes off himself. If you are depressed, and burned out, it's time to find a place of service and stop dwelling on yourself. Never give up, and don't give in. The church has too many sitting in the grandstands of life watching others on the field of battle because at some point they decided to quit.

I Need a Break!

Through the years, I've had many people confide, "Pastor, I am tired, I am worn out and I need a break." Like Elijah hiding in a cave wanting to die, they pull back and say, "Things are just too hectic in my life right now, so you won't see me in church for a while."

I have watched men and women go from sitting in the front, to the middle, to the back of the church. It's as if to say by their body language, "I want to get as far away as I possibly can and still be here." I am not criticizing where you sit in church; that's not the point. But when burnout slowly takes over, our body language screams, "Don't come in my space, and don't tell me to get over it. I am miserable and right now my emotions tell me to give up."

If anybody had a right to feel this way it was the Apostle Paul. Yet, I find no evidence that Paul ever experienced it. You may be thinking, "Why would Paul ever have to deal with the issue of burnout? After all, he was personally called and commissioned by

Jesus. He had it made, and has no idea of the things that I face." Really? Consider this:

In Acts 20 we read about Paul preaching all night in Troas, then leaving by ship early the next day. I can find no mention of the apostle stopping to rest. Without a doubt, this was not the only time Paul conducted all night teaching services. Although he listed in 2 Corinthians 11:23-29 many tough experiences, he found joy and expressed encouragement for others.

The care of just one church plunges some ministers into burnout, but Paul refers to his daily care of *all* the churches.

What was Paul's secret?

The apostle knew if he tried to minister in his own strength (the flesh) he would end up shipwrecked and on the trash heap of history. How did he avoid it? He gives insight to his secret in the following statement: *"I have been crucified with Christ and I no longer live, but Christ lives in me. The life I now live in the body, I live by faith in the Son of God, who loved me and gave himself for me"* (Galatians 2:20 NIV).

Paul determined the best approach was to exchange his weak flesh for the strength of the Holy Spirit.

Read the book of Acts and his epistles. Paul shares many striking statements that sustained him in the most difficult situations:

- *"None of these things move me"* (Acts 20:24).
- *"But thanks be to God, who always leads us as captives in Christ's triumphal procession and uses us to spread the aroma of the knowledge of him everywhere"* (2 Corinthians 2:14).
- *"So we fix our eyes not on what is seen, but on what is unseen, since what is seen is temporary, but what is unseen is eternal"* (2 Corinthians 4:18).
- *"For Christ's love compels us, because we are convinced that one died for all, and therefore all died"* (2 Corinthians 5:14).
- *"I die daily"* (1 Corinthians 15:31).

- *"Night and day we pray most earnestly that we may see you again and supply what is lacking in your faith"* (1 Thessalonians 3:10).
- *"Be filled with the Spirit"* (Ephesians 5:18).
- *"When I am weak, then am I strong*" (2 Corinthians 12:10).
- *"This one thing I do"* (Philippians 3:13).
- *"To live is Christ, and to die is gain"* (Philippians 1:21).
- *"I have learned to be content"* (Philippians 4:11).
- *"I can do all things through Christ"* (Philippians 4:13).
- *"In everything give thanks"* (1 Thessalonians 5:18).

Pastor Daniel R. Vess gives this advice on regaining your spiritual spark:

> *There is a positive side to Spiritual Burnout. It is a warning signal to the Christian to awaken and rekindle their passion for their first love. Like a hot air balloon when the flame burns out we begin to drift down toward destruction. When the flame burns hot and bright we soar higher toward heaven and closer to God.*
>
> *Every Christian and every congregation needs to work hard to revive its spiritual spark. The story was told about the church house that was on fire and the preacher, the elders and a few members came to put out the fire. A man across the street also came to help. After the fire was out, one of the elders thanked the man and said, "I don't believe I've seen you before."*
>
> *The man replied, "No you haven't." "But why, you only live across the street". "Because this church has never been on fire before." Remember, spiritual zeal is contagious. There is nothing more impressive or attractive than a church full of Christians on fire for the Lord.*

Instead of running on empty, stay constanty filled with the Spirit.

CHAPTER 7

THE GREAT EXCHANGE

The old cross slew men; the new cross entertains them. The old cross condemned; the new cross amuses. The old cross destroyed confidence in the flesh; the new cross encourages it.
– A. W. TOZER

Without God's provision for our sin it would not be possible for us to live in abundance and blessing. An amazing event took place over 2,000 years ago that changed everything. It's called, *The Miracle of Exchange.*

Exchange means, "To give or to take in return for another thing." Or, "The act of giving and receiving."

We need to understand how this system works. Many wait for years for something to happen and it never does. They become discouraged, confused, and give up. They pray and cry, and yet nothing materializes. Why? They don't understand that God's kingdom is about exchange.

I'm not referring to bribing or making a deal with God. The Almighty is not our personal servant, nor our butler.

A large part of the Christian experience consists of exchanging something worse for something better. The yoke of Jesus deals with every aspect of our lives. When He asks us to come to Him with our burdens and promises to give us rest (Matthew 11:28), the Lord is offering an exchange. He is saying, "I will take your heavy yoke of bondage in exchange for my yoke of forgiveness, freedom, and a better way of life."

Here are just a few of the life-transforming exchanges the Lord offers:

- My weakness for His strength (Isaiah 40:31).
- My death for His life (Galatians 2:20).
- My sadness for His joy (Isaiah 61:1-3; John 15:11).
- My lack of understanding for His wisdom (James 1:5).
- My emptiness for His fullness (Ephesians 3:19).
- My sickness for His healing (Isaiah 53:4-5).
- My poverty for His riches (2 Corinthians 8:9).

But, there is one exchange that must take place *first*:

My sin for His righteousness.

"And giving joyful thanks to the Father, who has qualified you to share in the inheritance of his holy people in the kingdom of light. For he has rescued us from the dominion of darkness and brought us into the kingdom of the Son he loves, in whom we have redemption, the forgiveness of sins" (Colossians 1:12-15 NIV).

Sin Created Self-Consciousness

"God made him who had no sin to be sin for us, so that in him we might become the righteousness of God" (2 Corinthians 5:21 NIV).

The word "sin" in this verse not only refers to what we would normally think of as "religious errors," but includes everything in our lives that falls short of the glory of God's original design (See Romans 3:23).

If you want to see this design, look back to the Garden of Eden. There you will find a man and a woman living in unbroken fellowship with Father God. They were untouched by sickness, grief, or poverty—and they exercised dominion over the whole earth. When God created man, He didn't place him just anywhere without thought; He created an ideal environment called Eden.

Myles Munroe, in his book, *The Purpose and Power of Praise and Worship,* sheds light on this topic:

The root in Hebrew of the word Eden is uncertain. The Greek version of the Old Testament, the Septuagint, relates the word to the Hebrew verb eden or ayden, which means delight. Therefore, Eden is translated as the garden of delight. Other occurrences of the word Eden in the Old Testament equate Eden with the garden of the Lord. (See Isaiah 51:3 and Ezekiel 28:13.)

Thus, God prepared a garden for man, an environment where it was pleasant and where His presence touched the earth. This is why the Bible never says that Adam planted the garden. Rather, God was the one who planted the garden. That is, God came and impressed (planted) His presence in the earth."

The Creator prepared a perfect, pleasant environment and His presence permeated the earth. Eden was a place of continual fellowship between God and His creation (Adam). It was the Lord's plan for how He wanted us to live. It would be fair to say the ideal setting to fulfill purpose is nothing more and nothing less than the presence of God Himself—which was the Creator's greatest gift to Adam.

THERE IS TROUBLE IN PARADISE

Now the serpent was more crafty than any of the wild animals the Lord God had made. He said to the woman, "Did God really say, 'You must not eat from any tree in the garden'?" The woman said to the serpent, "We may eat fruit from the trees in the garden, but God did say, 'You must not eat fruit from the tree that is in the middle of the garden, and you must not touch it, or you will die.'"

"You will not certainly die," the serpent said to the woman. "For God knows that when you eat from it your eyes will be opened, and you will be like God, knowing good and evil."

When the woman saw that the fruit of the tree was good for food and pleasing to the eye, and also desirable for gaining wisdom, she took some and ate it. She also gave some to her husband, who was with her, and he ate it. Then the eyes of both of them were opened, and they realized they were naked; so they sewed fig leaves together and made coverings for themselves (Genesis 3:1-7 NIV).

This was the snake, the father of lies. He had already tried to "one up" God by ascending to the throne. This was, of course, Satan's ultimate ambition when he was Lucifer, God's angelic servant: *"How you have fallen from heaven, morning star, son of the dawn! You have been cast down to the earth, you who once laid low the nations! You said in your heart, 'I will ascend to the heavens; I will raise my throne above the stars of God; I will sit enthroned on the mount of assembly, on the utmost heights of Mount Zaphon. I will ascend above the tops of the clouds; I will make myself like the Most High"* (Isaiah 14:12-14 NIV).

Satan is a created being, a creature; but he wanted to be worshiped and served like God. This attitude of rebellion led him to seek to establish his own kingdom. When that didn't happen, he worked his deceit on Eve. If he couldn't one-up God, he would lure the woman into doing it for him!

What was Satan's target?

His first attack was against her mind. *"But I am afraid that just as Eve was deceived by the serpent's cunning, your minds may somehow be led astray from your sincere and pure devotion to Christ "* (2 Corinthians 11:3 NIV).

The reason Satan wants to target your mind is because it is where God communicates and reveals His will to you. The Lord renews our lives by renewing our minds, and He does this through His truth. "Sanctify them by the truth; your word is truth" (John 17:17 NIV).

Your thought process affects your whole being. Like a computer, it can store facts and impressions, even emotions—and recall those details years later. Your mind can reach into the past through memory, or it can reach into the future through imagination. Your thinking affects your feeling and your will. Remember, *"For as he thinks in his heart, so is he"* (Proverbs 23:7 NKJV).

Satan knows the tremendous power of your mind, and he tries to capture it for himself. If the devil can convince you a lie is the truth, then he can begin his deceit that leads you into sin. We must protect our thoughts from the attacks of the father of lies. Paul warns that if something is not true, we should not allow it entrance into our beings. Instead, *"...whatever is true, whatever is noble, whatever is right, whatever is pure, whatever is lovely, whatever is admirable—if anything is excellent or praiseworthy —think about such things"* (Philippians 4:8 NIV).

What were Satan's tactics?

The devil came to Eve as the subtle deceiver. Revelation 12:9 names him the *"serpent of old who is called the Devil and Satan, who deceives the whole world."*

Notice the tactics the devil used in the Genesis account to cause Eve to believe his lie:

1. He doubted God's word. "Indeed, has God said?"

Satan did not deny God had spoken; he simply questioned whether God had really said what Eve thought He had. He suggested that maybe Eve misunderstood what she heard.

2. He denied God's word. "You surely shall not die!"

The devil took the small step from questioning to denying. Remember, Adam and Eve had never seen death, all they knew is what God told them. No doubt the Lord spoke with them concerning many things. I would've loved to have heard some of their conversations as God walked with them in the cool of the evening.

If Eve had not fallen into the serpent's trap of doubt, she would have never fallen into his trap of denial.

3. He disputed God's love. "If God really loved you, He wouldn't keep something from you."

Eve is about to make an exchange. She is about to trade perfect "oneness" for "likeness." Satan said, "You will be like God." The temptation was to convince Eve that the Creator was holding out on her. Adam and Eve were already made in the image of God, with all rights and privileges, including dominion over the earth. It's as if she thought likeness was a greater privilege than oneness. "You will be like God" is a gigantic lie that has controlled civilization since the fall of Adam and Eve.

As Paul warned the believers at Corinth, *"They exchanged the truth about God for a lie, and worshiped and served created things rather than the Creator—who is forever praised"* (Romans 1:25 NIV).

EVE'S THREE MISTAKES

How did Eve respond to Satan's attack? She made three mistakes that ultimately led her into sin.

Mistake #1: She misquoted God's permission.

In Genesis 3:2, Eve omitted the word "freely." God's original directive in Genesis 2:16 was, *"From any tree of the garden you may eat freely."*

Satan's subtle lie, "God is holding out on you!" is a tactic the enemy used on her. It was so subtle you can pass right by and not see it. When she began to question the goodness and grace of the Lord, it was much easier to disobey His clear instructions.

Mistake #2: She misquoted God's prohibition.

We do not find the words, "or touch it," in the original command. There is no record of God ever telling them what Eve says in verse 3. Eve not only made the Creator's original command less gracious by omitting the word "freely," but she also made the prohibition more grievous by adding "or touch it."

Satan is always trying to convince us that God's commands are a burden and he can offer something better. Another gigantic lie! (See 1 John 5:3).

Mistake #3: She misquoted God's penalty.

God did not utter the words, "Lest you die." Once again we have to look at the original command in Chapter 2:17, *"For in the day that you eat from it you shall surely die."*

Eve changed God's word! The scheme of the enemy was to convince Eve that the penalty for her disobedience would not be as harsh; therefore, she could consider turning away from God's will and obeying Satan's desires.

WARNING!

If we treat our heavenly Father's commands in this manner, we leave ourselves wide open for deception. Look what Satan did to Eve. He merely permitted her to consider the tree apart from what God had said. I can almost hear the enemy whisper, "Look at the tree. It is good for food, delightful to the eyes, and will make one as wise as God."

It was time for Eve to make a choice: God's word or Satan's lies? She rejected God's command, took the tempting bait from the devil, and sinned. Disobedience always has consequences. Eve was not alone. She brought Adam into her web of deceit, and for the first time they realized they were naked.

Until this moment, they were without clothes, but now their eyes were taken off the Creator and onto themselves. Before, they were God-conscious and now they are self-conscious!

I like the description of author Arthur W. Pink: "Satan is ever seeking to inject that poison into our hearts to distrust God's goodness—especially in connection with His commandments. That is what really lies behind all evil, lusting and disobedience. A discontent with our position and portion, a craving from something which God has wisely held from us. Reject any suggestion that God is unduly severe with you. Resist with the utmost abhorrence anything that causes you to doubt God's love and His loving-kindness toward you. Allow nothing to make you question the Father's love for His child."

The downward spiral of Adam and Eve continued as they tried to cover their sin with fig leaves. When God asked Adam, "Where are you?" He was not inquiring because He didn't know, rather because He wanted Adam to realize what had happened. Before that moment, they were so God-conscious they were only aware of Him. Sin stole that away and made them conscious of themselves.

As a result, we have been suffering from the consequences of Eve's decision ever since. When the first Adam ate from the Tree of the Knowledge of Good and Evil, his original sin was imputed onto all of mankind.

SELF-CONSCIOUSNESS ALWAYS LEADS TO SELF-CENTEREDNESS

What started in the garden with Satan's attempt to "one-up" God did not end with Adam and Eve. Because sin entered, all of humanity is born with the same nature toward each other.

Remember Samson?

A perfect example is found in the Old Testament. In judges 14 we are introduced to Samson. The Bible calls him a hero, but he's really a spoiled brat. Like a pampered child who thinks the whole world revolves around him or her, Samson thought he could do anything he wanted and have whatever he desired.

His story (Judges 13) starts with great expectation. Samson's mother was barren. She was visited by an angel who told her she would bear a son who would be a *"Nazirite to God from the womb; and he shall begin to deliver Israel out of the hand of the Philistines"* (verse 5).

As we look at his life, we discover that in reality he never did any such delivering. Why? Because Samson never delivered himself.

Numbers 6 describes three commitments a Nazirite must keep during the period of his vow:

1. Avoid any contact with grapes or the drinking of wine.
2. Never touch a dead body of any kind.
3. Let your hair grow and never get it cut.

Samson's downfall started with marrying a woman his parents disapproved of. Like a petulant child, he had to have what he wanted. At the marriage feast, he played a joke by giving a riddle to 30 Philistine men. They wagered 30 linen garments. Since the men couldn't figure it out, they went to his bride and convinced her to find the answer to the riddle—threatening to burn her family out of house and home if she wouldn't help them. She pulls the age old trick on Samson with, "If you really love me you would tell me the answer."

Smitten by her, Samson shared the answer and had to pay his bet of 30 garments. "*Then the Spirit of the Lord came powerfully upon him. He went down to Ashkelon, struck down thirty of their men, stripped them of everything and gave their clothes to those who had explained the riddle. Burning with anger, he returned to his father's home*" (Judges 14:19 (NIV).

Meanwhile back at the feast:

> *Later on, at the time of wheat harvest, Samson took a young goat and went to visit his wife. He said, "I'm going to my wife's room." But her father would not let him go in. "I was so sure you hated her," he said, "that I gave her to your companion. Isn't her younger sister more attractive? Take her instead."*
>
> *Samson said to them, "This time I have a right to get even with the Philistines; I will really harm them." So he went out and caught three hundred foxes and tied them tail to tail in pairs. He then fastened a torch to every pair of tails, lit the torches and let the foxes loose in the standing grain of the Philistines. He burned up the shocks and standing grain, together with the vineyards and olive groves* (Judges 15:1-5 NIV).

The real story here is that Samson's bride was given away. Such an act of betrayal would hurt any man's ego. He then had a negative change in attitude, thinking, "Don't blame me for what I'm about to do!"

Samson's feats are legendary, but it is his flaws that proved to be fatal. His two major weaknesses were revenge and romance. In fact, his passion for women often led him on the road to revenge. He was extremely gifted, but certainly not godly. He was strong on the outside, but had no control on the inside. Samson developed a problem. Some would say that he had a "roving eye."

As a result, Samson did not fight according to God's plan. He was mad, angry, and hurt, and was taking his hostility out on the Philistines.

Many people suffer with "spiritual roving eyes." They are constantly looking around for something new. Every time the enemy realizes that God is about to move you to the next level, he will place a distraction in your path. Often, it is something from your past. Please don't make "today's" decisions based on "yesterday's pain."

Samson never recovered from what happened to his first wife.

Now his enemies knew his Achilles' heel. They knew he "liked" the women, and used that weakness against him:

- The enemy is looking for an opening.
- Don't help him out.
- Keep your single vision/integrity intact.
- Whatever is not healed in you will kill you.
- Whatever is "catching your eye" at the moment is the very thing that can rob your passion.
- Samson was living with division. He had a divided heart.
- He had two agendas: trying to live for God, and still carrying around bitterness and hate that he was taking out on the enemy.
- If you are not at peace with yourself, you will never be at peace with anyone.

SAMSON'S STORY IS OUR STORY

We can read the accounts of Hannah, Gideon, or Ruth and think, "I could never be like them." Not so with Samson. He's much like you and me. Most of us know what it means to be tempted. At times, we all wrestle with the desire for revenge.

We've been there, we understand. So when we read of Samson struggling and falling, we have an idea of what he was going through. The truth of the matter is that there's a little bit of Samson in all of us—and a whole lot in most of us. One of the things we learn from this man's life is that sin will always take us farther than we want to go.

He loved the wrong woman.

Scripture tells us, *"Sometime later, he fell in love with a woman in the Valley of Sorek whose name was Delilah. The rulers of the Philistines went to her and said, "See if you can lure him into showing you the secret of his great strength and how we can overpower him so we may tie him up and subdue him. Each one of us will give you eleven hundred shekels of silver"* (Judges 16:4-5 NIV).

The story is often told in books, sermons, and films that Samson's downfall was all about lust. Can you imagine having your sin portrayed on the big screen? He loved her. His attitude was, "I am not going to lose again. I will do everything I can to keep her."

Here he was, laying with a woman who wanted to kill him. Some people are so arrogant that they think they can play with fire and never get burned. Be warned. Anything that causes you to lose your vision, you need to run from.

He gave away the wrong thing.

Delilah coyly asked, "How can you say, 'I love you,' when you won't confide in me? This is the third time you have made a fool of me and haven't revealed the source of your great strength. *"With such nagging she prodded him day after day until he was sick to death of it. So he told her everything. 'No razor has ever been used on my head,' he said, 'because I have been a Nazirite dedicated to God from my mother's womb. If my head were shaved, my strength would leave me, and I would become as weak as any other man'"* (Judges 16:15-17 NIV).

First, he revealed his secret, which led him to give away his heart. Whomever you give your hidden thoughts to will have all of you. Out of the heart flow the issues of life.

His fatal flaw is exposed.

Samson's final romance ends in disaster. Delilah's name means "weakness" or "brought low." She certainly pulled Samson down! He gave his heart to her and became putty in her hands. The combination was lethal.

Samson's fatal attraction was based on sex. Delilah's motivation was for money. The Philistines were after power. This trifecta of money, sex, and power has brought many good people to their destruction. He disclosed his secret in order to save face.

After playing the "If you really loved me, you'd tell me" card, verse 16 informs us that she resorted to a war of words. She nagged and prodded him day after day *"until he was tired to death."*

Samson then told Delilah everything. Samson, was a fool. He wasn't tricked or deceived, but like Adam, he knew exactly what he was doing. The rulers of the Philistines came with the silver shekels in their hands, and Delilah put him to sleep on her lap.

Then it was too late. As soon as he fell sound asleep, Delilah called for a man to chop off his hair. Verse 19 says it plainly: *"His strength left him."*

The last phrase of verse 20 is one of the saddest statements in the entire Old Testament: *"But he did not know that the Lord had left him."*

Far too many Christians drift away from God through stupidity and folly, never realizing what they've done until it's too late. Even more tragic, they don't appreciate what they have until it's gone.

This entire episode started with a joke and ended in destruction! When you read the end of Samson's life you might think, "Well, at least he did something right before he died."

However, the tragedy is this: instead of being God's deliverer for the people, he became the source of sermons and movies about what *not* to do to accomplish your purpose. He is known more for his defeats than his victories!

CENTURIES LATER ANOTHER EXCHANGE TAKES PLACE

The most important Divine Exchange was prophesied by Isaiah, 700 years before it was fulfiled. God inspired him to write, *"All we like sheep have gone astray; we have turned, every one, to his own way; and the Lord has laid on Him the iniquity of us all"* (Isaiah 53:6).

Bible scholars agree that Isaiah was pointing to Jesus. The phrase "has laid" means to "meet together." The word used for "iniquity" means "rebelliousness." When you combine both of these, we see that God made all of the evil consequences of our rebellion to "meet together" on Jesus. This involves more than one act of sin. It really means that man has decided to "go his own way" without any regard for God or His Son. True rebellion is nothing more and nothing less than "doing our own thing!"

Some might protest that it is unfair for the wrongdoing of another person to also be treated as our own error. But by the same token, the "right doing" of Jesus has also become our "right doing."

When Jesus hung on the cross, a divinely ordained exchange took place. The God/Man, Jesus, who knew no sin, took upon Himself all the iniquity and evil that should have been mine (and yours).We justly deserved the wrath of God. But, because of what He did, we can now through faith receive all the blessings that were due to the perfect Son of God.

> *As for you, you were dead in your transgressions and sins, in which you used to live when you followed the ways of this world and of the ruler of the kingdom of the air, the spirit who is now at work in those who are disobedient. All of us also lived among them at one time, gratifying the cravings of our flesh and following its desires and thoughts. Like the rest, we were by nature deserving of wrath.*
>
> *But because of his great love for us, God, who is rich in mercy, made us alive with Christ even when we were dead*

> *in transgressions—it is by grace you have been saved. And God raised us up with Christ and seated us with him in the heavenly realms in Christ Jesus, in order that in the coming ages he might show the incomparable riches of his grace, expressed in his kindness to us in Christ Jesus.*
>
> *For it is by grace you have been saved, through faith—and this is not from yourselves, it is the gift of God—not by works, so that no one can boast* (Ephesians 2:1-9 NIV).

At Calvary, Jesus dealt a death blow to self-centeredness, selfishness, and rebellion.

The cross stands outside the dimension of time, and all the sins of all mankind: present, past, and future were placed upon the body of Jesus. As a Man walking the earth, God's Son enjoyed a very intimate relationship with His Father. But when all the sins of the world were imputed upon Him, the Father had no choice but to turn away from the Son. At that moment, Jesus experienced separation from God. That is why He could not refer to Him as Abba ("Father") but as Eloi "God." As it is recorded in Mark 15:34, *"And at the ninth hour Jesus cried out in a loud voice, 'Eloi, Eloi, lama sabachthani?'—which means, 'My God, my God, why have you forsaken me?'"*

British preacher, Frederick W. Robertson, describes it in musical terms: "The deep undertone of the world is sadness—a solemn bass, occurring at measured intervals and heard through all other tones. Ultimately, all the strains of this world's music resolve themselves into that tone. And I believe that the cross, and the cross alone, interprets the mournful mystery of life, the sorrow of the Highest—the Lord of Life, the result of error and sin, but ultimately remedial, purifying and exalting."

Jesus had to experience separation from God at the cross so that you and I can now enjoy complete intimacy with Him—without having to be afraid of Him! The Apostle Paul writes, *"For you did not receive a spirit that makes you a slave again to fear, but you received the Spirit of sonship. And by him we cry, "Abba, Father"* (Romans 8:15).

When we are born again, the Holy Spirit Himself comes and indwells us, so we no longer need to fear God. We can now address Him the same way Jesus did, by referring to Him as Abba Father (or Daddy God).

The final words of Jesus on the cross were, *"It is finished"* (John 19:30). This is translated from one single word in Greek, *teleo,* which means "to accomplish or to make complete."

"May I never boast except in the cross of our Lord Jesus Christ, through which the world has been crucified to me, and I to the world" (Galatians 6:14 NIV).

In the words of an unknown writer, "If you were to look at Rembrandt's painting of The Three Crosses, your attention would be drawn first to the center cross on which Jesus died. Then as you look at the crowd gathered around the foot of that cross, you'd be impressed by the various facial expressions and actions of the people involved in the awful crime of crucifying the Son of God. Finally, your eyes would drift to the edge of the painting and catch sight of another figure, almost hidden in the shadows. Art critics say this is a representation of Rembrandt himself, for he recognized that by his sins he helped nail Jesus to the cross."

Most of us have understood only a tiny fraction of what was accomplished at the Great Exchange called Calvary. It was the most complete event that has ever taken place. God left nothing out—not one cursed thing that came about through mankind's rebellion was left standing.

Jesus triumphed over all!

CHAPTER 8

WHERE ARE YOUR SPLINTERS?

Forgiveness is the fragrance the violet sheds on the heel that crushed it.
– MARK TWAIN

Author and Pastor Warren Wiersbe, in his insightful book, *Encouragement for Difficult Days,* describes an encounter he had with a gentleman in his church. It reminded him of the importance of forgiveness:

> *Recently I chatted with a man who was nervous, physically ill, and disturbed emotionally. I felt he should visit a specialist, but he wanted to talk to me, so I patiently listened. As his story came out, I began to understand why he was so miserable: he was long on memory and short on forgiveness. He remembered every unkind thing anybody had ever said or done to him. At times his eyes blazed with murderous anger. Once more I was reminded of the importance of forgiveness as one of the greatest spiritual medicines in all the world.*

Jesus, as a Rabbi with Semicha, had the authority to interpret the Torah. He often illustrated truth through parables. There were many times He answered questions from His disciples, or from the curious crowd, by telling them a story. This was His way of teaching His yoke (the body of interpretation of the law), and raising traditional teachings to a higher level. It should not come as a surprise that those listening to His words would exclaim, "We have never heard anyone teach like You, because You teach as one with authority" (See Mark 1:22).

THE DIFFERENCE BETWEEN DOING AND KNOWING

There is a fundamental contrast in the mindset of the Hebrews of biblical times, and the Western, Hellenistic way of thinking, out of which has emerged a large part of Christian belief systems.

In writing on "The Hebrew Mind vs. the Western Mind," scholar Brian Knowles makes these observations:

> *William Barrett, explains that one of the most fundamental differences between the Western, Hellenistic mind and the Hebrew mind is found in the area of knowing vs. doing. Says Barrett, "The distinction arises from the difference between doing and knowing. The Hebrew is concerned with practice, the Greek with knowledge. Right conduct is the ultimate concern of the Hebrew, right thinking that of the Greek. Duty and strictness of conscience are the paramount things in life for the Hebrew; for the Greek, the spontaneous and luminous play of the intelligence. The Hebrew thus extols the moral virtues as the substance and meaning of life; the Greek subordinates them to the intellectual virtues, the contrast is between practice and theory, between the moral man and the theoretical or intellectual man."*
>
> *This helps explain why so many Christian churches are focused on the issues of doctrinal orthodoxy (however they may define it)—often at the expense of godly living. In many Christian circles, what one believes or espouses is treated as more important than how one lives—i.e. how one treats his or her neighbor.*
>
> *In Biblical Judaism, it is precisely the opposite. Christians are inclined to subject each other to litmus tests of orthodoxy, while Jews are concerned mainly with behavior.*

It was gentile Christians, influenced by Greek philosophy, who both intellectualized and systematized Christian doctrine. Worse, they radically changed much of it. The Biblical Hebrews, and the Apostolic Era of the Church, had no formal theology as such. Nothing was systematized. The believing community had no entrenched hierarchy or magisterium through which all doctrine had to be filtered and approved. As with the unbelieving Jews, opinions varied from sage to sage.

MORE THAN "HEARERS"

Scripture gives us this instruction: *"But be doers of the word, and not hearers only, deceiving yourselves"* (James 1:22).

The Greek word for "hearers" is *akroatai*. It denotes more than our English term to "hear" something. It means those who listen with real interest, being very attentive—do so to increase knowledge, which brings a measure of satisfaction.

This word is used to describe an "auditor" at a university. We also get "auditorium" from this Greek term.

Who is an auditor, and what does that person do?

- One who sits with other students, has the same advantage in learning but doesn't have the same responsibilities. If you walked into the classroom, you couldn't distinguish who was an auditor.
- When exams are given they don't take them. The person doesn't have to be checked by the professor as to what he or she has learned. No term papers are required.
- An auditor feels liberated when he sees other students sweating it out. He knows that he is in the clear.
- The cost of the class is much less, no sacrifice is involved.

However, there is a down side. When the person who sat for the exams receives a diploma, the auditor gets nothing!

Some schools may give an auditor a piece of paper saying they attended the class, but that's about all.

In life, the most difficult individual to deal with is the person who loves to listen, does so with rapt attention, but never shoulders any responsibility.

The "hearer only" James describes is the one who enjoys all the benefits of grace but will not carry any of the obligations of grace. We know them as men and women who make no commitment to the church.

Let's face it. There is a certain feel of responsibility and accountability when you place yourself under the covering of a local body of believers. Sadly, many houses of worship have become nothing more than seminary classrooms where the class (congregation) is taught more on how to conjugate Greek verbs than how to live a godly life. Some congregations have become audiences watching a show, instead of an army being equipped to change the culture.

Paul encountered the same attitude in Acts 17:18-21:

> *Then certain Epicurean and Stoic philosophers encountered him. And some said, "What does this babbler want to say?" Others said, "He seems to be a proclaimer of foreign gods," because he preached to them Jesus and the resurrection. And they took him and brought him to the Areopagus, saying, "May we know what this new doctrine is of which you speak? For you are bringing some strange things to our ears. Therefore we want to know what these things mean."*
>
> *For all the Athenians and the foreigners who were there spent their time in nothing else but either to tell or to hear some new thing.*

These were professional "hearers"—and our churches are filled with them. It happens every Sunday. People walk through the doors and, by looking at them, you can't tell the difference between the "auditors" and the "doers." The only way you can know is to see who will shoulder the responsibility of carrying the burden and the work God has given us.

His Yoke Teaches a Different Way

In, Jesus' day, when the crowds listened to His parables, they were not looking for information, but for a revelation on a better way of life. A Hebrew would always ask himself, "Who am I in this story Jesus is telling; and what application does this have to my journey?"

In Matthew 18, Jesus gave one of the most dramatic parables of His ministry. It is the Parable of the Unforgiving Servant.

It is important that we not just hear what the Lord says, but we need to put ourselves into the story. In these last days, we desperately need what Jesus was teaching.

As the chapter begins, it seems that His disciples had more desire for honor than the real meaning of being a follower of Christ. They wanted to know, *"Who...is the greatest in the kingdom of heaven?"* (verse 1).

Jesus did not start an argument with them over the issue. Instead, He called a young child to sit in their midst and explained that the greatest would be *"whoever humbles himself as this little child"* (verse 4).

Then, after teaching on humility (verses 1-14) and honesty (verses 15-20), Jesus tackles a most difficult subject: forgiveness.

No doubt Peter had been listening to what the Master was saying, all the while asking himself, "Who am I in this story? What meaning does this have for me?"

"Then Peter came to Him and said, 'Lord, how often shall my brother sin against me, and I forgive him? Up to seven times?' Jesus said to him, "I do not say to you, up to seven times, but up to seventy times seven" (verse 21).

Jesus Introduces a New Math

It seems that Peter was very concerned over the number of times he would have to forgive. The Torah said you had to forgive three times for the same offense. Peter, being humble and magnanimous, declared he was willing to go above the law, "I will forgive seven times!"

Maybe Peter thought Jesus would look at him with admiration and say, "Oh, Peter, you are so benevolent and kind. I am so proud of you. Your humility overwhelms Me."

Instead Jesus looked at him and replied, "How about 490 times?" You see, Peter was posing the wrong question. He should have been asking how many times do I *get* to forgive, not how many times do I *have* to forgive.

Peter must have been shocked by the answer he received. Jesus was trying to make a point. Peter was asking for limits and measures, but Jesus was trying to teach him that where there is love there can be no limits or dimensions of forgiveness.

Love *"keeps no record of wrongs"* (1 Corinthians 13:5 NIV). In essence, by the time we forgive as often as Jesus asked, we enter into the *habit* of forgiving.

By the same token, to tell someone, "Just forget about it" and move on sounds easy, but it is one of the hardest things to do. God did not build us with an erase button to eliminate painful memories and past hurts.

When Paul said, "Forgetting those things which are behind," he was not suggesting a case of spiritual amnesia. The word "forget" literally means not to be influenced any longer. When the enemy brings up painful memories just to harass us, it is possible to be no longer swayed by our emotions. The memory may never disappear, but the emotional trauma can be healed.

- Are you thinking of someone right now who if you saw at Walmart you would turn and walk in the other direction?
- Is there a name that pops into your mind that triggers an emotional upheaval in your heart?
- Is there a person in your past who hurt you so deeply, all you can think about is how to get even?

If any of these things are true (and they probably are for most of us), the parable Jesus gave is what we need to hear.

Nowhere in His Matthew 18 teaching does Jesus imply a careless or shallow forgiveness. That may be the yoke of modern-day purveyors of a watered-down, cotton-candy gospel which teaches you can act and live anyway you want. Nor is it the yoke of Jesus to condemn and judge everyone who falls or messes up. The yoke of Jesus teaches love and forgiveness—and it triumphs over condemnation and judgment. To forgive is a choice of the will, not an emotional response to a singular event.

The power of unconditional forgiveness is seen in this story. Please note that this parable is not about salvation, for redemption is totally a work of grace and given without condition to anyone who is willing to repent and trust Christ as Savior. To make God's forgiveness a temporary thing is to violate Scripture (See Romans 5:8; Ephesians 2:8-9; Titus 3:3-7).

This story concerns forgiveness between brothers, not between unbelievers and God. It's about us—you and me—forgiving one another.

The main character in this drama went through three stages:

Stage One: He Was a Debtor (Matthew 18:23-27).

"Therefore the kingdom of heaven is like a certain king who wanted to settle accounts with his servants. And when he had begun to settle accounts, one was brought to him who owed him ten thousand talents. But as he was not able to pay, his master commanded that he be sold, with his wife and children and all that he had, and that payment be made. The servant therefore fell down before him, saying, 'Master, have patience with me, and I will pay you all.' Then the master of that servant was moved with compassion, released him, and forgave him the debt."

It was audit time at the company. This man had been stealing funds from his boss (the king), and it was a day of reckoning. The total tax levy in Palestine was approximately 800 talents a year, so you can guess how much he was stealing. In terms of today's money it would be the equivalent of millions of dollars.

He was caught red-handed and had nowhere to run. So he decided the best thing to do was to throw himself on the mercy of his employer. This man actually thought he could get out of paying the debt. Crazy as it may sound, he told the king if he were given enough time he could pay what he owed. It's obvious this man was not sorry for his crime; rather, he was ashamed because he got caught.

This individual was in a hopeless, dire situation. Fortunately for him, the king was a man of mercy and compassion. He assumed the loss, forgave the servant, and set the man and his family free. Just imagine the burden that was lifted from his shoulders when he realized that he and his family would not be thrown into a debtor's prison!

I know you can see the obvious truth. The servant did not deserve forgiveness; it was purely an act of love and mercy on the part of the king.

Stage Two: He Was a Creditor (verses 28-30).

Jesus continued the parable: *"But that servant went out and found one of his fellow servants who owed him a hundred denarii; and he laid hands on him and took him by the throat, saying, 'Pay me what you owe!' So his fellow servant fell down at his feet and begged him, saying, 'Have patience with me, and I will pay you all.' And he would not, but went and threw him into prison till he should pay the debt."*

Immediately after receiving compassion from the king, this man went out and found a fellow servant who owed him 100 pence. The average worker earned one penny a day (in current value around $3,200). Compared to what the servant had stolen from *his* master, which was canceled, you can see this debt from his fellow servant was chump change.

Instead of showing the same spirit of forgiveness he had received, he grabbed his friend and demanded the money be paid. The poor servant who owed such a small amount used the same approach as the one who was forgiven such a large debt. He cried "Just be patient with me, I will pay back all of it!"

But the hard-hearted servant was unwilling to give what he had demanded from others. It's true, he had the legal right to throw this man in prison, but he did not have the moral right. Why? Because he and his family had been spared the shame and suffering of imprisonment, why wouldn't he do likewise for his friend?

Stage Three: He Became a Prisoner (verses 31-34).

"So when his fellow servants saw what had been done, they were very grieved, and came and told their master all that had been done. Then his master, after he had called him, said to him, 'You wicked servant! I forgave you all that debt because you begged me. Should you not also have had compassion on your fellow servant, just as I had pity on you?' And his master was angry, and delivered him to the torturers until he should pay all that was due to him."

Upon hearing the news, the king became outraged. His servant had been delivered from prison, but by his own actions he was still under bondage. It's almost as if the king said, "You went out and exercised justice instead of mercy. So if you want to live by justice I will put you behind bars and let you suffer for your lack of compassion." The king decided to do to him what he had done to others.

Prison is not a place you volunteer to go. I've been told by those who have been incarcerated that existence behind bars is not really living at all. Losing your freedom is one thing, but no longer having the free will to make choices about your life is another. I am convinced the world's worst jail is not found in some Third World country, it's the prison of an unforgiving heart.

Jesus makes it clear in this parable that unforgiveness imprisons us and causes torment. Some of the most miserable individuals in the world are people who refuse to pardon others. They live with the idea that unforgiveness and bitterness is punishing the offender when, in fact, they're only inflicting pain on themselves.

As you read the parable, you may be thinking, "What was wrong with this man?" Well, it's the same thing that's a problem with many professing believers today. When we are unable to forgive those who have wronged us, it is an indication that we have never really experienced forgiveness deep in our hearts.

I find that many pray for personal grace and pardon, but when it comes to others we want to see justice without mercy. Such an attitude always brings torment and places us in a virtual penitentiary. But if we live according to forgiveness, giving to another what we have received ourselves, then we will enjoy the freedom that is ours in Christ.

Jesus closes the parable with a stern warning: *"So My heavenly Father also will do to you if each of you, from his heart, does not forgive his brother his trespasses"* (Matthew 18: 35).

Remember, the theme of this parable is forgiveness between brothers, not salvation for lost sinners. Jesus did not say that God only saves those who offer forgivness. The warning is: the Lord cannot pardon us if we do not have humble and repentant hearts. We reveal the true condition of our innermost being by the way we treat our fellow man. We gladly forgive others when our lives are filled with joy because we have been forgiven, but where there is pride and a desire for revenge, there can be no true repentance—therefore, God does not forgive us.

It is simply not enough to receive the Lord's forgiveness or even receive the pardon of someone else; we must experience it personally so it will make us gentle and compassionate toward those who have hurt us. As Paul writes, *"Bear with each other and forgive one another if any of you has a grievance against someone. Forgive as the Lord forgave you"* (Colossians 3:13 NIV).

Author Don Ratzlaff shares a story that was first told in the book, *Miracle on the River Kwai*:

> *The Scottish soldiers, forced by their Japanese captors to labor on a jungle railroad, had degenerated to barbarous behavior, but one afternoon something happened. A shovel was missing. The officer in charge became enraged. He demanded that the missing shovel be produced, or else. When nobody in the squadron budged, the officer got his gun and threatened to kill them all on the spot...It was obvious the officer meant what he had said.*
>
> *Then, finally, one man stepped forward. The officer put away his gun, picked up a shovel, and beat the man to death. When it was over, the survivors picked up the bloody corpse and carried it with them to the second tool check. This time, no shovel was missing. Indeed, there had been a miscount at the first check point. The word spread like wildfire through the whole camp. An innocent man*

had been willing to die to save the others!...The incident had a profound effect...The men began to treat each other like brothers.

When the victorious Allies swept in, the survivors, human skeletons, lined up in front of their captors (and instead of attacking their captors) insisted: "No more hatred. No more killing. Now what we need is forgiveness."

Sacrificial love has transforming power.

The yoke of Rabbi Jesus gives more insight into forgiveness and unconditional love by telling another illustration in Matthew 5. If you want to live like a king's kid, learn how to gain authority by demonstrating generosity (unconditional forgiveness).

In the words of Jesus, *"You have heard that it was said, 'Eye for eye, and tooth for tooth.' But I tell you, do not resist an evil person. If anyone slaps you on the right cheek, turn to them the other cheek also. And if anyone wants to sue you and take your shirt, hand over your coat as well. If anyone forces you to go one mile, go with them two miles. Give to the one who asks you, and do not turn away from the one who wants to borrow from you"* (Matthew 5:38-42 NIV).

In this passage, the teaching of God's Son is admittedly very challenging:

- It is opposed to what we have always been taught.
- We are called upon to be *"partakers of the divine nature"* (2 Peter 1:4).
- We are challenged to be more like God than men.

In order to be truly "sons of your Father in heaven," Jesus teaches a standard of righteousness that far exceeds:

- That of the scribes and Pharisees.
- That of the modern church.
- That of the majority of people today.

Pastor Scott L. Harris recounts this story:

Some years ago a man named Lucien had served the state of Kentucky "beyond the call of duty." One day he discovered that an old boyhood friend named Sam was serving time in the state penitentiary and had 8 more years to serve. Lucien went to the warden and asked if he could visit Sam, to which the warden agreed.

Lucien and Sam talked for two hours with their time ending with much laughing over some of the things that had happened in their youth. A month later Lucien visited the Governor and said: "I haven't been able to sleep. Sam, my boyhood buddy, is in prison. He was a good boy, Governor, and since you told that if there was anything Kentucky could do for me to name it, I came here to ask if a pardon might be granted. I'll take him into my business and into my home, for he has no family, and I have a big house."

A week later the Governor sent for Lucien and said: "Here's the pardon, but it's yours under one condition; that is, that you sit down in the warden's office and talk with Sam for two more hours. Then if you think you should give him the pardon, take Sam home. I will parole him to you."

Lucien hurried over to the penitentiary and again they sat down in the warden's office. Lucien said, "Sam, when you get out of here, will you go into business with me? I might even get you out of here sooner than you expect."

Sam got up and walked around awhile, looked out of the window, then said, "I don't believe I could accept that invitation, for I've got something to do when I get out of here, something very important. I'm going to do it just as soon as I get out of here."

"What is it, Sam?" Lucien asked. Sam turned around, the fire glinted from his eyes, hatred filled his whole face as he said, "I am going to get two men together—the judge who sent me up here and the witness—and I'm going to

kill them both with my bare hands."

Lucien left and tore up that pardon.

Such is the desire for revenge in man. Sam lost the opportunity for a pardon because his heart was full of hatred desiring only revenge. But revenge comes in less graphic forms as well, such as in the story of the old pious, but somewhat cranky old lady that had been inadvertently forgotten to be invited by her neighbors for a picnic. On the morning of the event they suddenly realized they had forgotten her and sent a little boy to ask her to come. "It's too late now," she snapped, "I've already prayed for rain."

The story in Matthew 5 of turning the other cheek is one of the most commonly misunderstood passages of Scripture. There is a tendency to take it out of its context and try to figure out what it really means. Through the centuries these verses have been used to promote lawlessness, anarchy, conscientious objection to military service, and even to the extreme that believers should be doormats and pushovers.

A proper interpretation of any Scripture depends upon its total framework. Jesus is contrasting true righteousness with pride and self-righteousness. He is simply describing the character of a changed heart. His yoke is always emphasizing the spirit of the law as opposed to traditional rabbinic teaching. In each illustration, He contrasts His yoke with that of the scribes.

Just Punishment vs. Revenge

The scribes were famous for twisting the Mosaic Law. "Eye for eye and tooth for tooth" is found in the Old Testament in three places: Exodus 21:24, Leviticus 24:20, and Deuteronomy 19:21. The law required just punishment to someone who had committed a crime. It was a restriction demanding a sentence to match the offence—and to keep vengeance from playing a part in punishment.

The scribes had distorted this law into meaning that when a person offended you, then you were required to take revenge on that individual. It was designed to prevent overkill—like killing a fly with an atom bomb!

Attacks on Personal Honor

Jesus' first illustration was to show that the evil committed against us are attacks on our personal honor: *"But whoever slaps you on your right cheek, turn the other to him also"* (Matthew 5:39).

In the cultural context, to slap someone in the face is a sign of disrespect. The fact that it is the right cheek would seem to be the common form of speaking, in which the right is generally before the left. However, it is interesting to note that in order for the right cheek to be struck, either the left hand would have to be used or the back of the right hand.

If the intent was to hurt you physically, you would be hit with a closed fist not an open hand. In Jesus' day, to be slapped was a terrible indignity. So when you turn the other cheek you are taking dominance over the individual who is insulting you. Every time you demonstrate forgiveness you gain authority over the one you forgave.

Attacks on Personal Property

The second illustration Jesus gives concerns personal protection which was afforded by the law. Jesus says, *"If anyone wants to sue you and take away your tunic, let him have your cloak also"* (verse 40).

The tunic was the inner garment and the cloak the outer garment.

If someone wanted to sue you, and proved their claim, if you had no other means, the court could demand that you pay off your debt with your clothing. The law required only the outer cloak could be taken as a commitment to pay. The law also stated that the cloak had to be returned by evening because it was his only covering.

Remember, if you gave both your outer and inner garments you would be naked. It was not a sin to be without clothes, however, it was a sin to see a person naked. So to give them all your clothing was to shame them for their lack of grace!

Jesus is telling us that a person who is truly righteous of heart will go above and beyond what is necessary and required in order not to cause offense with an adversary. Once again, by demonstrating forgiveness, He is taking authority over the individual who is the aggressor.

Attacks on Personal Freedom

Jesus' third illustration involves attacks on our individual liberty. *"And whoever compels you to go one mile, go with him two"* (verse 41).

Again, the cultural context sheds light on this statement. Israel was controlled by martial law, and the Roman government was in charge. They ruled the people by taxation and intimidation. It was not uncommon for a Roman soldier to compel a stranger to carry his pack, which could weigh up to 70 pounds. It's interesting that Roman law said they could only compel them to carry it one mile. To make a person carry it for two miles would be breaking military law and the soldier could be court-martialed.

Imagine how resentful you would be if you had to carry a soldier's heavy load, expecially if it were that of an occupying army who was your dreaded enemy. Once again, Jesus is teaching a better way. To walk the extra mile is to demonstrate grace and forgiveness.

The Apostle Paul summarizes what Jesus teaches: *"Do not repay anyone evil for evil. Be careful to do what is right in the eyes of everyone. If it is possible, as far as it depends on you, live at peace with everyone. Do not take revenge, my dear friends, but leave room for God's wrath, for it is written: 'It is mine to avenge; I will repay,' says the Lord. On the contrary: 'If your enemy is hungry, feed him; if he is thirsty, give him something to drink. In doing this, you will heap burning coals on his head.' Do not be overcome by evil, but overcome evil with good"* (Romans 12:17-21 NIV).

Have you been mistreated, insulted, lied about, or abused? When you look at the cross of Jesus, it is God saying, "So have I, and, Oh, by the way, I lost a Son in the process!"

The last words of dying men are very revealing:

- Karl Marx drew his last breath on March 14, 1883. His housekeeper said, "Tell me your last words and I'll write them down." Marx replied, "Go on, and get out! Last words are for fools who haven't said enough!"
- Circus master P.T. Barnum said as he was dying, "What were today's receipts?"
- The last words of the great Baptist preacher, Charles Spurgeon, were, "Jesus died for me."
- John Wesley, the founder of Methodism, uttered, "The best of all is, God is with us."

Consider the dying words Jesus said from the cross. Seven times He spoke, but His first statement opens a window that enables us to look into eternity and see the heart of God: *"Father, forgive them; for they know not what they do"* (Luke 23:34).

The Greek New Testament indicates that Jesus repeated this prayer over and over again. As they pounded the nails into His hands and feet, He prayed, "Father forgive them." When they lifted the wooden cross and dropped it into the hole in the ground, Jesus prayed again, "Father, forgive them."

He could have cried, "Father, judge them; bring punishment and retribution on them." He could have called for legions of angels to deliver Him, but He did not. Why did He pray this way? Jesus was simply practicing the very message that He preached. He taught the yoke of forgiveness, and told the people, "If you don't forgive from your heart, God cannot forgive you."

To be a disciple of Jesus we must understand the meaning of Calvary. Jesus said, *"And whoever does not carry their cross and follow me cannot be my disciple"* (Luke 14:27 (NIV).

The Divine Miracle of Grace

In his widely acclaimed book, *My Utmost for His Highest, Oswald Chambers writes:*

Beware of the pleasant view of the fatherhood of God: God is so kind and loving that of course He will forgive us. That thought, based solely on emotion, cannot be found anywhere in the New Testament. The only basis on which God can forgive us is the tremendous tragedy of the Cross of Christ. To base our forgiveness on any other ground is unconscious blasphemy. The only ground on which God can forgive our sin and reinstate us to His favor is through the Cross of Christ. There is no other way! Forgiveness, which is so easy for us to accept, cost the agony at Calvary.

We should never take the forgiveness of sin, the gift of the Holy Spirit, and our sanctification in simple faith, and then forget the enormous cost to God that made all of this ours.

Forgiveness is the divine miracle of grace. The cost to God was the Cross of Christ. To forgive sin, while remaining a holy God, this price had to be paid. Never accept a view of the fatherhood of God if it blots out the atonement. The revealed truth of God is that without the atonement He cannot forgive—He would contradict His nature if He did. The only way we can be forgiven is by being brought back to God through the atonement of the Cross. God's forgiveness is possible only in the supernatural realm.

Compared with the miracle of the forgiveness of sin, the experience of sanctification is small. Sanctification is simply the wonderful expression or evidence of the forgiveness of sins in a human life. But the thing that awakens the deepest fountain of gratitude in a human being is that God has forgiven his sin. Paul never got away from this. Once you realize all that it cost God to forgive you, you will be held as in a vise, constrained by the love of God.

If you and I have taken up the cross to follow Jesus it means we recognize that when He died, our sin nature was crucified with Him. As it is written:

> *What shall we say, then? Shall we go on sinning so that grace may increase? By no means! We are those who have died to sin; how can we live in it any longer? Or don't you know that all of us who were baptized into Christ Jesus were baptized into his death? We were therefore buried with him through baptism into death in order that, just as Christ was raised from the dead through the glory of the Father, we too may live a new life.*
>
> *For if we have been united with him in a death like his, we will certainly also be united with him in a resurrection like his. For we know that our old self was crucified with him so that the body ruled by sin might be done away with, that we should no longer be slaves to sin—because anyone who has died has been set free from sin.*
>
> *Now if we died with Christ, we believe that we will also live with him. For we know that since Christ was raised from the dead, he cannot die again; death no longer has mastery over him. The death he died, he died to sin once for all; but the life he lives, and he lives to God.*
>
> *In the same way, count yourselves dead to sin but alive to God in Christ Jesus. Therefore do not let sin reign in your mortal body so that you obey its evil desires. Do not offer any part of yourself to sin as an instrument of wickedness, but rather offer yourselves to God as those who have been brought from death to life; and offer every part of yourself to him as an instrument of righteousness. For sin shall no longer be your master, because you are not under the law, but under grace* (Romans 6:1-14 NIV).

Without question, when we carry a wooden cross, we are going to get splinters—and they are painful. Splinters are the cost for choosing to forgive. To carry the cross is a choice, as is the demonstration of grace and forgiveness to others who have hurt us. The power of the cross is working in those who choose to be a disciple of the Lord Jesus Christ.

It doesn't take much to imagine the body of Jesus being racked with splinters, especially since He was hung on a roughly hewn piece of wood. This was in addition to all the other physical pain and abuse He endured.

To follow Jesus is to carry a cross, and the more you bear the more splinters you receive. Splinters, like Jacob's limp, are reminders of the cost of discipleship (See Luke 14:28-33).

To forgive is painful, yet necessary to live a life of freedom.

- Splinters – Paul and Silas singing praises at the midnight hour.
- Splinters – Peter hanging upside down on a cross crying out, "Hold this not against them!"
- Splinters – Stephen being stoned, looking into an open heaven and praying, "Lord, do not charge them with this sin."
- Splinters – What we receive every time we carry the cross of forgiveness toward those who have hurt us.

"In him we have redemption through his blood, the forgiveness of sins, in accordance with the riches of God's grace" (Ephesians 1:7 NIV).

Where are your splinters?

CHAPTER 9

THE UNSTOPPABLE FORCE

God's unfailing love for us is an objective fact affirmed over and over in the Scriptures. It is true whether we believe it or not. Our doubts do not destroy God's love, nor does our faith create it. It originates in the very nature of God, who is love, and it flows to us through our union with His beloved Son.

– JERRY BRIDGES

One of my favorite words is *unstoppable*. Something is on the horizon, approaching at full speed, and there is nothing anyone can do to slow it down. Unstoppable—like a tornado, a tsunami, or a stampede.

When you read the pages of Scripture, it is evident that the love of God is the one force Satan could not stop. From Genesis through Revelation, the enemy was trying to become an immovable object to block the unstoppable love of God. The culmination of the devil's resistance was seen at the cross of Calvary.

The issue of the cross was not about trying to stop a man, it was Satan's attempt to abort the message of unconditional love. Without question, when Jesus hung on the cross all the forces of Hell were celebrating victory. All they needed to hear was one word from the lips of Jesus to condemn those who were unjustly crucifying Him. But instead of curses, they heard forgiveness!

The tsunami of God's love crested on top of Golgotha's hill, unleashing a tidal wave of love sweeping across the nations. The effects were so strong that the impact is still being felt today.

Let me share the light shed on this topic by Dave Scrivner in his web log, Word Traveler:

> *What happens when an irresistible force meets an immovable object? This popular dilemma is known as the Irresistible Force Paradox and unfortunately, there is no answer. Logically if there is such a thing as an irresistible force, then no object can be immovable. Vice versa, it is impossible for an irresistible force to exist if there is an immovable object anywhere in the vicinity. If both existed in the same universe, they would seek each other out for the ultimate showdown.*
>
> *The Irresistible Force Paradox naturally leads us to the question of the nature of God. It is similar to the Omnipotence Paradox illustrated by questions like "Can God create a rock so heavy that He cannot lift it?"*
>
> *The Chinese word for the word "paradox" literally means "spear-shield." The term originated from a 3rd century BC book entitled "Han Feizi" written by a Chinese philosopher of the same name. The book contains a story about a weapons vendor peddling a spear he claimed could penetrate any shield. Interestingly, he also had a shield for sale that was, apparently, strong enough to deflect any spear. I think you know where this story is going.*
>
> *So, what happens when an irresistible force meets an immovable object? Maybe both the force and the object surrender. Or, perhaps they exchange roles...the unstoppable force stops and the immovable object moves. The most plausible answer to me was posed by Victor Serebriakoff in one of his Mensa puzzle books...the Irresistible Force Paradox is truly "an inconceivable event".*
>
> *I love the mystery of the "inconceivable" nature of God. He is "the Rock of our salvation." God is both irresistible and immovable. Within Himself is contained the power of the unanswered paradox. He imagined and caused to happen many "inconceivable events" like the Creation of the world from nothingness, the Immaculate Conception of Mary, the Incarnation of the God-Man*

Jesus, and the Resurrection of the crucified Christ. None of this is possible or even fully imaginable to me. However, "the things that are impossible with people are possible with God" (Luke 18.27).

So as for me and my household, we will accept the divine paradox and "shout joyfully to the [irresistible and immovable] Rock of our salvation."

GOD TOOK THE FIRST STEP

God literally put everything on the line for us by offering His Son in sacrificial death. Love is a risky business, but the Almighty was willing to take that risk.

As it is described in the Message Bible, *"Christ arrives right on time to make this happen. He didn't, and doesn't, wait for us to get ready. He presented himself for this sacrificial death when we were far too weak and rebellious to do anything to get ourselves ready. And even if we hadn't been so weak, we wouldn't have known what to do anyway. We can understand someone dying for a person worth dying for, and we can understand how someone good and noble could inspire us to selfless sacrifice. But God put his love on the line for us by offering his Son in sacrificial death while we were of no use whatever to him"* (Romans 5:8 MSG).

What kind of love are we talking about? In the English language we use the same word to describe many things. For instance, we use the word love to express how we feel about our favorite cake, car, or our spouse. Not so in the Greek language.

In Greek, there are four primary words to describe the concept of love. Each convey a distinct type:

1. Eros

This is the Greek term for sexual love, from where we get our word erotic. In the culture of the day, this referred to casual impulses to satisfy or gratify the sexual desires of the flesh. This type of love is a demanding love, not one that seeks to give or please someone else.

2. Stergo

This word primarily pictures the love that exist between parents and children and members of the extended family. One scholar noted that on occasion, the word "stergo" demonstrates the love of a nation for its ruler or even the love of a dog for its master. The real root of this word is that of devotion.

3. Phileo

The best way to describe "phileo" is affection, such as fondness felt between two friends. It describes the idea of two or more people who are well suited and complementary to each other. Although it is a beautiful concept of love, it is not the highest form mentioned in the Bible.

4. Agape

Only found in the New Testament; *agape* is chiefly used to picture the love of God. Paul uses it in Galatians 5:22 when he says, *"But the fruit of the Spirit is love."*

THE CALL OF LOVE

In my studies, I have discovered that many Bible scholars and translators have had a hard time trying to explain the depth and meaning of the word *agape*. In one interpretation, "Agape occurs when an individual sees, recognizes, understands, or appreciates the value of an object or a person, causing the viewer to behold this object or person in great esteem, awe, admiration, wonder, and sincere appreciation."

The most recognized example of *agape* is found in John 3:16: *"For God so loved (agape) the world that He gave His only begotten Son, that whoever believes in Him should not perish but have everlasting life."*

I love how The Message Bible presents it: *"This is how much God loved the world: He gave his Son, his one and only Son. And this is why: so that no one need be destroyed; by believing in him, anyone can have a whole and lasting life. God didn't go to all the trouble of sending his Son merely to point an accusing finger, telling the world how bad it was. He came to help, to put the world right again. Anyone who trusts in him is acquitted; anyone who refuses to trust him has long since been under the death sentence without knowing it. And why? Because of that person's failure to believe in the one-of-a-kind Son of God when introduced to him*" (John 3:16-18 MSG).

Love in Action

Words without action are empty and meaningless. Real agape love requires a certain amount of risk. You literally put your heart on the line not knowing what kind of response you are going to receive in return.

When God looked at mankind, He stood in awe even though man was separated by sin. Humanity was held captive by Satan, however, God looked upon His creation and saw His own image. He loved man so deeply that His heart was stirred to do something to save him. In essence, God's love drove Him to action.

Agape is deep and profound. It knows no boundaries or limits, or how far, wide, high, and deep it will go to show that love to all who will receive it—even if it means sacrificing itself for the sake of that object or person it so deeply cherishes. Agape love is the highest form of love, a self-sacrificial type that takes action.

God's love has no strings attached. Man is self-centered, self-seeking, and will give love only if he can get something in return. Not so with our heavenly Father!

John, the apostle of love, writes in his letter: *"Dear friends, let us love one another, for love comes from God. Everyone who loves has been born of God and knows God. Whoever does not love does not know God, because God is love. This is how God showed his love among us: He sent his one and only Son into the world that we might live through him. This is love: not that we loved God, but that he loved us and sent his Son as an atoning sacrifice for our sins. Dear friends, since God so loved us, we also ought to love one another"* (1 John 4:7-11 NIV).

John makes it very clear that the love of God is genuine and real—focused on the object which is loved and not on itself. It is willing to take risk, to be hurt and wounded—because it is totally self-effacing and selfless in character.

"Jesus Loves Me"

There is no man, woman, or child too high or too low who cannot be touched by the love of God. Author Mitchell Dillon gives this example:

> *Whitney Houston, in an interview with Diane Sawyer in 2002, discussed the pain and frustration she experienced in her failed comeback attempt. At one point in the interview she turned to Ms. Sawyer and asked, "Have you ever heard the sound of 10,000 people disappointed in you?"*
>
> *Hailed as perhaps the greatest vocalist of all time, Whitney Houston once stood atop the music industry as the unchallenged queen of pop. The greatness of her talent was met by an equally magnanimous outpouring of love from millions of fans the world over. But when her abuse of drugs and other related habits finally robbed her of that "golden voice," the cheers turned to jeers.*
>
> *She had risen to the pinnacle of admiration like few others, only to have it all melt away as soon as her flaws were revealed. The rejection left her confidence wavering from the resonating sound of her fans' disapproval. Even so, in that same interview, Ms. Houston declared emphatically, "I know this—Jesus loves me!" It was a declaration she would assert repeatedly, even at the occasion of her final public appearance the night before she died.*
>
> *Despite her flaws and self-doubt, there was one thing she did not question: the love of Jesus. What a critical realization, one which highlights the important distinction between the love of the world and the love of God. The former is fickle and fleeting; the latter is sure and eternal. If an adored star like Whitney Houston could suffer the pain of this world's fickle love, don't think it won't treat you the*

> *same—or worse! The sad truth is we must conceal our flaws if we hope to hang on to the love of this world. But not so with the love of God! His love is felt most strongly when we lead off with them!*

"And we have known and believed the Love that God has for us. God is love, and he who abides in love abides in God, and God in him" (1 John 4:16).

Why would the Father go to such lengths to save us? If all we understand about the price paid for our redemption is that it saves us from hell so we can go to heaven when we die, we have missed the majority of the yoke of Jesus—which included three- and-a-half years of teaching and His sacrificial death.

If the issue of salvation did not involve heaven or hell, would Jesus still be worth following? Is His path a better way of life? The answer is yes!

With every slap to His face, with every stripe on His back, with every spike driven in His body, God was dealing a death blow to a fruitless and empty religion. The Lord did not pay the ultimate cost to save us from hell, no; He did it to save us from ourselves!

On one hand, religion (man's attempt to save himself by works), was screaming condemnation, judgment and hopelessness. On the other hand, God took a risk and demonstrated unconditional love. And now He says to all nations: *"The Spirit and the bride say, 'Come!' And let the one who hears say, 'Come!' Let the one who is thirsty come; and let the one who wishes take the free gift of the water of life"* (Revelation 22:17 NIV).

Contrary to His usual manner of ministry, Jesus demonstrated two acts of judgment: He cleansed the temple, and cursed a fig tree. Let's examine what happened in the temple at Jerusalem:

> *Jesus entered the temple courts and drove out all who were buying and selling there. He overturned the tables of the money changers and the benches of those selling doves. "It is written," he said to them, 'My house will be*

called a house of prayer,' but you are making it 'a den of robbers.'"

The blind and the lame came to him at the temple, and he healed them. But when the chief priests and the teachers of the law saw the wonderful things he did and the children shouting in the temple courts, "Hosanna to the Son of David," they were indignant.

"Do you hear what these children are saying?" they asked him. "Yes," replied Jesus, "have you never read," 'from the lips of children and infants you, Lord, have called forth your praise'?" And he left them and went out of the city to Bethany, where he spent the night (Matthew 21:12-17 NIV).

Whose house is it anyway?

In just three short years, hollow religion had degenerated from *"a house of merchandise"* (John 2: 16), to *"a den of robbers"* (verse 13). Bible historians tell us that Annas, the former high priest, was the overseer of this lucrative business, assisted by his sons. The purpose of the court of the Gentiles in the temple was to give the "outcast" an opportunity to learn about the true God from Israel. What started out as a convenience for visitors soon turned into a money making operation. Price gouging was the norm, not the exception. The purveyors of exorbitant prices eliminated their competition and if anyone dared to oppose them, they were dealt with severely. It was their equivalent of a first century mafia enterprise. If television had been available in those days it would've made a hit reality show. A first century version of the Sopranos!

It may sound harsh, but look at what the Son of God did: *"Jesus went straight to the Temple and threw out everyone who had set up shop, buying and selling. He kicked over the tables of loan sharks and the stalls of dove merchants. He quoted this text: My house was designated a house of prayer; you have made it a hangout for thieves"* (Matthew 21:12-13 MSG).

As far as I can tell, this is the only time Jesus became angry. A visual demonstration of empty religion drove Him to this action. The court of the Gentiles was used for mercenary business, not missionary business, and Jesus would have none of it.

By declaring this was "My house," He was affirming He was God. He was quoting from Isaiah 56:7: *"...these I will bring to my holy mountain and give them joy in my house of prayer. Their burnt offerings and sacrifices will be accepted on my altar; for my house will be called a house of prayer for all nations"* (NIV). The entire chapter of Isaiah 56 condemns the unfaithful leaders of Israel.

In Jeremiah 7, the prophet gives a long sermon at the gate of the temple, rebuking the people for the same sins that Jesus saw and judged in His day. The phrase "den of robbers" is a direct quotation from Jeremiah 7:11: *"Has this house, which bears my Name, become a den of robbers to you? But I have been watching! Declares the Lord"* (NIV).

Based on a misunderstanding and misinterpretation of what Jesus was actually doing, there are some who say that it's inappropriate to have merchandise for sale in a church. The Lord was not judging whether or not it is acceptable to sell things in God's house; that was not the point. He called the temple a "den of robbers" because the place where robbers hide is called a den. The leaders were using the temple as a cover-up for their sins.

Thankfully, when empty religion is kicked out, His house becomes a house of:

- **Prayer** – *"My house shall be called a house of prayer"* (Matthew 21:13).
- **Power** – *"The blind and the lame came to Him in the temple, and He healed them"* (verse 14).
- **Praise** – *"But when the chief priests and scribes saw the wonderful things that He did, and the children crying out in the temple and saying, 'Hosanna to the Son of David!' they were indignant and said to Him, 'Do you hear what these are saying?' they asked him. And Jesus said to them, 'Yes. Have you never read, "Out of the mouth of babes and nursing infants You have perfected praise"?'"* (verses 15-16).

TIME FOR ANOTHER OBJECT LESSON

> *And he left them and went out of the city to Bethany, where he spent the night. Early in the morning, as Jesus was on his way back to the city, he was hungry. Seeing a fig tree by the road, he went up to it but found nothing on it except leaves. Then he said to it, "May you never bear fruit again!"*
>
> *Immediately the tree withered. When the disciples saw this, they were amazed. "How did the fig tree wither so quickly?" they asked. Jesus replied, "Truly I tell you, if you have faith and do not doubt, not only can you do what was done to the fig tree, but also you can say to this mountain, 'Go, throw yourself into the sea,' and it will be done. If you believe, you will receive whatever you ask for in prayer"* (Matthew 21:17-22 NIV).

It may come as a surprise that Jesus would curse an innocent tree, but once again, the Lord was giving a visual demonstration of empty fruitless religion.

Jesus was close to Jerusalem in the last week of His public ministry. The fig tree incident was only one day after He kicked out the mercenaries who were taking advantage of the people. Christ was showing the difference between dead religion and a living relationship with God.

Have you ever wondered why Jesus chose a fig tree and not some other tree? Why didn't he curse an oak, or an olive tree?

Before we discuss the matter, we need to understand "the law of first mention." This principle simply stated is: when something is mentioned the first time in the Bible it will mean the same every other time throughout Scripture.

When were fig leaves first noted in the Bible? You have to go all the way back to the Garden of Eden to apply the law of first mention. *"Then the eyes of both of them were opened, and they realized they were naked; so they sewed fig leaves together and made coverings for themselves"* (Genesis 3:7 NIV).

- Sin was introduced to man for the very first time.
- Sin separated them from God.
- Sin broke their relationship with the Creator.
- Sin brought condemnation and guilt.

Until that time, Adam and Eve didn't know what sin was. They had no idea of condemnation and guilt. But on this day, they felt the terrible consequences of sin and death. Their joy was replaced with sadness and guilt. Their peace was replaced with fear and condemnation. Their contentment was replaced with anxiety. The eyes of them both were opened and they discovered the folly of disobeying God. They could discern between good and evil, yet had no power to do anything about it. The consequence was confusion and shame.

Before they sinned, they were delighted to see their Maker, but after their transgression they did not want anything to do with Him. Sin causes us to want to hide from God physically, emotionally, and spiritually because we know we are guilty. Their oneness with the Almighty was replaced by a self-centered attitude.

To conceal their guilt and shame, fig leaves were sewn together as a covering for their nakedness. Somehow they thought they could hide from God among the trees of the garden. Man has been trying to hide this way for thousands of years.

The fig leaf represents man's attempt to make himself approved to God. It didn't work for the first humans and it will not work for us. We all have become very creative when it comes to fig leaves.

Some try:

- Hiding behind the fig leaves of tradition.
- Hiding behind the fig leaves of good works and service.
- Hiding behind the fig leaves of trying to keep the Ten Commandments.
- Hiding behind the fig leaves of mom and dad's religion.

A person once said, "The oldest profession is not what people think; it is the clothing industry. We are constantly trying to cover up."

In the case of Adam and Eve, *"The Lord God made tunics of skin and clothed them"* (Genesis 3:21). However, before they sinned, He warned, *"...but of the tree of the knowledge of good and evil you shall not eat, for in the day that you eat of it you shall surely die"* (Genesis 2:17). The Bible declares, *"The wages of sin is death"* (Romans 6:23), and *"The soul who sins will die"* (Ezekiel 18:20). Spiritually, Adam and Eve died the moment they sinned. In time, they died physically.

God was going to give the first visual demonstration of His love by clothing them with the skins of two dead animals, probably lambs. Adam and Eve were guilty and deserved immediate death, but God chose innocent animals to die in their place. The shedding of blood of an innocent creature was a picture of another who would one day shed His blood on behalf of sinful man. Jesus was *"The Lamb of God who takes away the sin of the world!"* (John 1:29).

The only death that can possibly deal with sin is the death of God's son. His blood alone can cleanse us from all iniquity (Hebrews. 9:22; 1 John 1:7,9). There is no other detergent that will wipe away our guilt (1 Peter 1:18-19; Revelation 5:9).

God's perfect covering for sin is the blood of the Lamb of God. Fig leaves will never suffice for what God alone can do. The Father's provision is through the death of His Son, Jesus Christ. The choice has always been between "leaves or skins."

SEARCHING FOR FRUIT

Jesus was walking from Bethany back to Jerusalem when He noticed a fig tree by the side of the road. But as He drew closer, He saw there was no fruit—just leaves. This is when He cursed it and said, "May you never bear fruit again." The tree withered and died.

Fred Wright, in his book, *The Barren Fig Tree,* makes this observation: "The normal habit of the fig tree is that fruit begins to form on the tree as soon as leaves appear. Leaves and fruit also disappear together. It was said of this fig tree which Jesus and his disciples saw, 'for the time of the figs was not yet' (Mark 11:13). Actually this was no excuse for this fig tree, because if this was not the time for figs, it was also not time for the leaves to appear. By a show of leaves, it was like many people, pretending to have fruit which was not there. *The fig tree was advertising fruit—but was empty."*

THE FOUR LESSONS OF THE FIG TREE

When the disciples saw what happened, *"they marveled, saying, 'How did the fig tree wither away so soon?' So Jesus answered and said to them, 'Assuredly, I say to you, if you have faith and do not doubt, you will not only do what was done to the fig tree, but also if you say to this mountain, "Be removed and be cast into the sea," it will be done. And whatever things you ask in prayer, believing, you will receive'"* (Matthew 21:20-22).

By this visual demonstration of cursing the fig tree, Jesus was teaching His disciples four important lessons:

1. The fig tree symbolized the nation of Israel.

"I will take away their harvest, declares the Lord. There will be no grapes on the vine. There will be no figs on the tree, and their leaves will wither. What I have given them will be taken from them" (Jeremiah 8:13 NIV).

"When I found Israel, it was like finding grapes in the desert; when I saw your ancestors, it was like seeing the early fruit on the fig tree. But when they came to Baal Peor, they consecrated themselves to that shameful idol and became as vile as the thing they loved" (Hosea 9:10 NIV).

2. The call of love is to confront dead religion.

Faith and love show the real difference between a fruitless religion and a relationship with the living God. Jesus said to His disciples, if they have faith and do not doubt they will be able to recognize the difference between empty religion, which produces no fruit, and a real relationship with God which is from the inside out.

3. The challenge of faith is to deal with mountains.

In the background of this demonstration was the Temple Mount. It was a symbol of a lifeless religion that produced no fruit. The traditional teaching is to speak to the mountains (a symbol of problems and difficulties that we face), but that is not what Jesus was talking about. No doubt He was looking at the Temple Mount and said, "This mountain has disregarded My glory and My purpose for coming into the world. It has turned its back on the unconditional love of God. It has turned religion into an empty shell with no power—a fig tree with leaves, but no fruit!"

4. Faith without doubting can cast the mountain of His love into the sea.

When a Hebrew heard the word "sea" he knew it was a symbol of humanity. Jesus was teaching them to speak to the mountain, not of dead religion, but to the mountain of His glory and unconditional love. Jesus was telling them, "The message of My gospel will save the whole earth!"

The theme of the modern church is, "Me, me! What about me?" The call of love says, "It's not about me. It's about Him."

To cast the mountain of His unconditional love into the sea (nations) of lost humanity means that we are willing to take the risk to be hurt, rejected, and abused. This is what Jesus did for us. He was willing to take the suffering and the shame of the cross in order to demonstrate His eternal love. The cross was His way of asking us to marry Him even before He knew our answer. This is faith and love in action!

THE COST OF LOVE

"When Jesus had finished saying all these things, he said to his disciples, 'As you know, the Passover is two days away—and the Son of Man will be handed over to be crucified'" (Matthew 26:1-2 NIV).

The final act in this cosmic confrontation is about to come to a climax. The full expression of unconditional love is about to be demonstrated for the whole world to witness, and it's going to come at a heavy price.

In one of his sermons, pastor Ian Sweeney shared this story:

> *One summer day in 1937 John Griffith, controller of a railroad drawbridge across the Mississippi, took Greg, his eight-year-old son with him to work. About noon, John raised the bridge to let some ships pass while he and Greg ate their lunch on the observation deck.*
>
> *At 1:07 p.m. John heard the distant whistle of the Memphis Express. He had just reached for the master lever to lower the bridge for the train, when he looked around for his son Greg. What he saw made his heart freeze. Greg had left the observation tower, slipped and fallen into the massive gears that operated the bridge. His left leg was caught in the cogs of the two main gears.*
>
> *With the Memphis Express steaming closer, fear and anxiety gripped John as his mind searched for options, but there were only two. He must either sacrifice his son and spare the passengers on the Memphis Express, or sacrifice them to spare his son. Burying his face in his left arm, John, with an anguished cry, pulled the master switch with his right hand to lower the bridge into place.*
>
> *Lord knows what anguish John Griffith had to go through, whichever decision he made. But I know this: God values us enough to sacrifice His Son that we too might live.*

For more than three years, Jesus had taught the people, and His message so often centered on lifting the yoke of religious bondage. Now He was going to die for them.

The pressure Jesus faced during His ministry was enormous:

1. He was subjected to spiritual abuse.

Jesus was betrayed by a trusted member of His inner circle. I don't know what price you would place on your soul, but Judas was an easy mark; he charged but thirty pieces of silver.

When numbers are given in the Bible, they always have significance. The number thirty in Hebrew is "Lamid" which means "friend of Yahweh"—and it is the number of divine order.

Judas was not the victim of circumstances or a puppet. It was prophesied that one of the Messiah's inner circle would betray Him (Psalm 41:9; 55:12-14). However, the fact that Judas was fulfilling prophecy does not relieve him of personal responsibility.

2. He was subjected to physical abuse.

Jesus was arrested, mocked, and tortured by the Roman authorities. The soldiers undressed Jesus and placed an old "soldier's coat" around Him. They said a king must have a crown, so they wove together thorns and pushed it into His scalp. They spat in His face, hit Him with a stick, and pulled the hair from His face.

Jesus endured the humiliation and pain without a word. His submission was not a sign of weakness; it was a sign of strength! They fashioned a whip, commonly known as a cat-o'-nine-tails. The ends were made of metal and pieces of bone that ripped the flesh away from the muscle. Historians tell us that seven out of ten prisoners died at the whipping post.

3. He was subjected to emotional abuse.

Jesus was deserted, disowned, and denied by His closest friends. The writer of Proverbs says, *"Faithful are the wounds of a friend"* (Proverbs 27:6). God's Son certainly knew the reality of that statement.

THE CHALLENGE

The ultimate challenge of unconditional love is, "Can you forgive those who have hurt, abused, and denied you?"

No doubt the one who hurt Jesus the most was Peter. The denial by this disciple of ever knowing Christ was the climax of a series of failures. Jesus warned Peter that he would be tested.

Instead of listening to the Master's words, Peter, full of pride, said he would remain true and never leave His side. Peter's boastfulness landed him in trouble before, but this time it was the ultimate failure.

> *Afterward Jesus appeared again to his disciples, by the Sea of Galilee. It happened this way: Simon Peter, Thomas (also known as Didymus), Nathanael from Cana in Galilee, the sons of Zebedee, and two other disciples were together.*
>
> *"I'm going out to fish," Simon Peter told them, and they said, "We'll go with you." So they went out and got into the boat, but that night they caught nothing. Early in the morning, Jesus stood on the shore, but the disciples did not realize that it was Jesus. He called out to them, "Friends, haven't you any fish?"*
>
> *"No," they answered. He said, "Throw your net on the right side of the boat and you will find some." When they did, they were unable to haul the net in because of the large number of fish* (John 21: 1-6 NIV).

After His resurrection, Peter had a private meeting with Jesus (Mark 16:7; 1 Corinthians 15:5). This was when God's Son made the decision to restore him publicly.

It's been said that the best way to learn life lessons is through the pressure cooker of trials. There is an old saying, "A Christian is like a tea bag, no good until it is put in hot water!"

Peter is a prime example. He learned the importance of paying attention to the Word, staying awake when watching and praying, and by never putting confidence in his own strength.

Without question, the apostle became totally convinced in the reality of the resurrection, but there was one thing of which he was not sure—that the Lord Jesus would ever use or trust him again.

Peter decided to go back to his old way of life. His shame and brokenness led him to the conclusion, "What's the use of staying here, I'm going fishing." The rest of the group responded, "If that's the case, we're going with you" (See John 21:3).

Early the next morning Jesus stood on the shore (they didn't know it was Him) and called out to them, *"'Friends, haven't you any fish?' "No," they answered. He said, 'Throw your net on the right side of the boat and you will find some.' When they did, they were unable to haul the net in because of the large number of fish"* (John 21:5-6).

I have the suspicion that the Lord told all the fish to hide! Peter and his friends couldn't catch the first smallest minnow. But Jesus instructed them to try fishing from the right side of the boat. Now the right side was the wrong side to cast your net, because the net would be backwards.

This was another illustration from Jesus. He was telling them that they couldn't make things work with their own ability or ingenuity! The wrong side is always the right side when Jesus is in control.

When Peter and his friends reached shore, they finally realized it was Jesus. I'm sure everything about the breakfast encounter reminded Peter of his failure. Although Jesus never brought up the past, all Peter had to do was look around:

- The Sea of Galilee was the same place he first met Jesus, fishing.
- Simon Peter smelled the smoke from the fire of coals and it reminded him of the last time he was near a charcoal fire; when he denied knowing Christ.
- When he saw bread, Peter must have remembered when Jesus took bread and fed five thousand.

After the meal was finished, Jesus questioned Peter three times concerning love. There is a difference in the Greek text that is not apparent in the English version. Jesus used the word "agape" for love, while Simon Peter responds with "phileo" (the Greek word for affection—or "like").

With that distinction, here is how John 15:21 should be interpreted: "Simon, do you love Me?" Peter responded, "Lord, You know I like You." All presumption and pride is gone. The second time, "Simon, do you love Me?" "Lord, You know I like you."

The third time, however, Jesus asked, "Simon, do you like

(phileo) Me?" It was as if the Lord was saying, "I'll meet you right where you are because I'm going to convert you with unconditional love."

The Bible says Simon was grieved and replied "Lord You know all things, You know I like you. Then Jesus told him, "All right, feed My sheep." Three times the Lord asked Peter that question in order to heal the disciple's three earlier denials.

The conclusion of the matter is this: "Simon Peter, I know you have failed. You have been tested, sifted, but I've got something for you to do. I am not through with you."

When you flip a few pages in the Bible, you'll see the same man preaching on the day of Pentecost. The man who was made of shifting sand is now a solid rock. Peter was no longer wavering, but standing with courage to preach the death burial and resurrection of Jesus Christ and call men to repentance!

The same Jesus who made a rock out of Peter is saying to us, "Follow Me and I will make you what you were meant to be."

Unconditional love forgives and heals past failures. His unstoppable love points you to a future filled with hope and purpose.

The yoke of Rabbi Jesus is always a better way!

All God's plans have the mark of the cross on them, and all His plans have death to self in them.

– E. M. BOUNDS

CHAPTER 10

THE LAST FULL MEASURE

If Jesus Christ be God and died for me, then no sacrifice can be too great for me to make for Him.

– C. T. STUDD

Invited to speak at the consecration of a memorial honoring the dead at Gettysburg, Abraham Lincoln, on November 19, 1863, delivered one of the most well-known speeches in American history.

While the address is extremely short—just 267 words—Lincoln used the opportunity both to honor the sacrifice of the soldiers and to remind American citizens of the necessity of continuing to fight the Civil War. The Gettysburg Address stands as a masterpiece of persuasive rhetoric. To me, the most memorable line is: "..that from these honored dead we take increased devotion to that cause for which they gave *the last full measure of devotion."*

Two years later, after Lincoln was killed, U. S. Senator Charles Summer commented on this memorable speech and in his eulogy of the slain president, called it a "monumental act." He said Lincoln was mistaken that "the world will little note, nor long remember what we say here." Rather, the Bostonian remarked, "The world noted at once what he said, and will never cease to remember it. The battle itself was less important than the speech."

Lincoln's address was masterful, and the death of the soldiers on the battlefield was honored.

In reality, however, no speech and no sacrifice could ever compare to the sacrifice of God's Son. The day Christ died was the ultimate act of "the last full measure of devotion."

IN THE EYE OF THE STORM

Matthew 26 and 27 sheds light on the climax of this confrontation between law and love, religion and redemption. It compares five separate but connected events.

Event #1: Jesus is at Bethany: the contrast between worship and waste (Matthew 26:1-16).

While the religious leaders were conspiring to kill Jesus, those who loved Him were demonstrating their love by hosting a dinner in His honor. Most Bible scholars agree there were seventeen people at this meal: Simon, Mary, Martha, Lazarus, Jesus, and the twelve apostles.

Let's look at the three main players:

Mary the Worshiper – the sister of Martha and Lazarus (verse 7).

Mary is only mentioned three times in the Gospels, and in each instance she is seen worshiping at the feet of Jesus. Combining all of the Gospel records concerning this event we learn that she anointed both His head and His feet with ointment, and wiped His feet with her hair.

According to Scripture, a woman's hair is a symbol of her glory. Mary's act of devotion filled the room with fragrance, which was her way of saying, "I surrender all to You." As an act of faith and pure love, she anointed His body before His death. I somehow believe that Mary knew Jesus would not need the traditional care after the crucifixion because Christ would not be in the tomb for very long!

Judas – the disciple no one really knew (verses 20–25).

Sounding like an ordinary church member, Judas began to criticize the waste of expensive ointment. His argument sounded so spiritual that it convinced everyone else he had to be right. "This is such a waste; the ointment could have been sold and the money given to feed the poor." This sounds convincing, but the only problem with his assessment is that it was wrong!

Judas didn't really care about the poor; he wanted the money to go into the coffers of the treasury. After all, he kept the funds and was a trusted member of the group. But as we later find out, Judas was not who they thought he was. He was a fake, a fraud, the great pretender. Like many who frequent our churches, Judas was "in" the group of believers, but was not one "of" them.

Jesus – the Defender (verses 10-13).

The Lord defends Mary and rebukes the disciples. Mary's demonstration of love is a witness to the whole world that anything you do to serve and love Him is not a waste. Jesus was not teaching that they shouldn't be neglectful of the poor; He was warning them not to miss an opportunity to worship. His yoke said that the poor will always be with them, but the opportunity to worship and prepare Him for burial was right in front of their eyes.

Event #2: They gather to celebrate Passover: the contrast between darkness and light (Matthew 26:17-30).

As preparations were being made for the Passover feast, Jesus announced there was a traitor among them. The disciples were shocked and began to wonder who the person might be. Judas was not a prime suspect because Jesus treated him the same as everyone else.

While it is true that the Scriptures predicted the betrayal, Judas was not relieved of personal responsibility. He had every opportunity to back out of his scheme to betray Jesus for thirty pieces of silver. After the Lord gave Judas a morsel of bread—which is a sign of honor given by the host to the guest—Satan entered Judas and he went out to fulfill his treacherous deed.

When this darkness departed from the room, Jesus instituted something new: the Lord's Supper.

Event #3: Gethsemane: the contrast between agony and apathy (verses 31-56).

While Jesus' future was hanging in the balance, His most

trusted disciples, Peter, James, and John were sleeping. In the natural I can understand this, because wine was served at the meal. I've read that wine can be used as a sleep aid, much like being feeling sleepy on Thanksgiving after eating too much turkey. However, this is not a valid excuse, because danger was lurking in the shadows.

Facing the horrific death of crucifixion, Jesus needed His friends, and yet they valued sleep more than obedience to His instructions to "watch and pray."

Jesus, the God-Man was not resisting the Father's will in the Garden of Gethsemane, which means "oil press." He faced death with courage. The Lord was about to drink the cup that was prepared for Him before the foundation of the world. He would soon bear in His body the sins of all mankind! His disciples would forsake Him, deny Him, and at some point, His Father would have to turn His back on Him. Is it any wonder His agony led to sweating blood?

Many have questioned whether Jesus, in His agonizing prayer, actually sweat drops of blood, or was it a figure of speech?

This issue was addressed by Dr. David Miller, in his essay, "A Physician's View of the Crucifixion":

> *The observant viewer of Mel Gibson's movie, The Passion of the Christ, will note that in the garden scene, one manifestation of the agony of Jesus was the tiny blotches of blood that surfaced on His facial skin. This feature of Christ's suffering is alluded to by Luke, the author of the New Testament books of Luke and Acts, who himself, by profession, was a physician. His writings manifest an intimate acquaintance with the technical language of the Greek medical schools of Asia Minor.*
>
> *Of the four gospel writers, only Dr. Luke referred to Jesus' ordeal as "agony" (agonia). It is because of this agony over things to come that we learn during His prayer "his sweat was as it were great drops of blood falling down to the ground" (Luke 22:44). Only Luke referred to Jesus' sweat (idros)—a much-used term in medical language. And only Luke referred to Jesus' sweat as consisting of great*

drops of blood (thromboi haimatos)—a medical condition alluded to by both Aristotle and Theophrastus.

The Greek term thromboi (from which we get thrombus, thrombin, et al.) refers to clots of blood. Bible scholar Richard Lenski commented on the use of this term: " 'As clots,' thromboi, means that the blood mingled with the sweat and thickened the globules so that they fell to the ground in little clots and did not merely stain the skin."

We can conclude quite justifiably that the terminology used by the gospel writer to refer to the severe mental distress experienced by Jesus was intended to be taken literally—i.e., that the sweat of Jesus became bloody.

From these factors, it is evident that even before Jesus endured the torture of the cross, He suffered far beyond what most of us will ever suffer. His penetrating awareness of the heinous nature of sin, its destructive and deadly effects, the sorrow and heartache that it inflicts, and the extreme measure necessary to deal with it, make the passion of Christ beyond all comprehension.

Event #4: The arrest of Jesus: the contrast between His yoke, (the power of God), and the arm of the flesh (Matthew 26:47-56).

The arrest of Jesus was imminent, and again He used the occasion to teach His yoke. He was innocent, yet treated like a common criminal. The Son of God had committed no crime, yet He was about to face punishment only afforded to the worst of the worst.

Judas, and a band of soldiers (300 to 600), along with the temple guards, showed up to arrest the Son of God. As prearranged, Judas used a kiss to identify the Master, which was not necessary since Christ calmly surrendered to them.

It was customary for the disciples to kiss their Rabbi as a sign of love and affection. However, this was not a demonstration of devotion; Judas used the kiss as a weapon. The Greek verb used here for "kiss" means continuous action. He didn't kiss him on the cheek one time, but continued kissing Him repeatedly. Judas kissed the door of heaven and ended up in hell!

After this act of betrayal, Jesus stepped forward and asked the mob, *"Whom are you seeking?"* (John 18:4). They answered Him and said "Jesus of Nazareth."

When they heard the statement, *"'I am He,' they drew back and fell to the gound"* (verse 6).

The Lord did not identify Himself as Jesus of Nazareth, as they expected, instead He declared, *"I AM!"* Jesus had used that phrase to describe Himself before (John 8:58; John 13:19).

Every Hebrew in the crowd knew exactly what He was saying, because they immediately recognized those were the same words God used to identify Himself when He spoke to Moses on Mount Horeb (Exodus 3:14).

The mob came armed with weapons of violence to arrest Jesus, yet when He declared who He really was, they were knocked to the ground and overwhelmed by a blast of God's power!

Rick Renner, in his book, *Sparkling Gems from the Greek,* gives insight into those who "fell to the ground" when they came to arrest Jesus:

> *The words "went backwards" come from the Greek word "aperchomai." In this case, the words depict the soldiers and Temple police "staggering and stumbling backward," as if some force has hit them and is pushing them backwards. The word "fell" is the Greek word "pipto," which means to fall. It was used often to depict a person who fell so hard, it appeared that they fell dead or fell dead like a corpse.*
>
> *What a shock it must have been for those military men! They discovered that the mere words of Jesus were enough to overwhelm and overpower them! The tales they had heard about Jesus' power were correct. Of course He really was strong enough to overcome an army. After all, He was the great "I AM!"*

No one would have blamed Jesus if He had resisted—especially Peter, who was ready for a fight! The mob was coming at Jesus with swords and clubs. What did He do? The Lord restrained His friend and healed His enemy (Luke 22:51). He said to Peter, *"Put your sword in its place, for all who take the sword will perish by the sword"* (Matthew 26:52).

God's Son could have called on the protectors of His glory. Instead, He makes an interesting statement: *"Do you think I cannot call on my Father, and he will at once put at my disposal more than twelve legions of angels?"* (verse 53 NIV).

The word "legion" is a term that was used in the Roman military. A legion was at least 6,000 soldiers, although it's possible for the number to be higher. So how many would be available to come that night to handle the situation and rescue the King of glory? Based on the numbers; if one legion equals 6,000 angels, simply put, Jesus was telling them that 72,000 angels were ready and available to rescue Him. The combined strength of this heavenly host is beyond comprehension.

Jesus resisted the temptation to fight fire with fire, or the temptation to call the heavenly warriors to come to His aid. His mention of angels struck fear in their hearts, because their view was vastly different than our modern depiction of these heavenly beings. The Lord could have called on them, and the darkness of the garden would have been brightly lit by the guardians of His glory. It would have made Hiroshima look like a small Fourth of July fireworks party!

Today, if you listen to Hollywood and not the Bible, angels are pictured as beautiful, bright white little fairies floating around and helping people. For example: *Touched by an Angel, Angel on my Shoulder, Angels in the Outfield*—or any other depictions in movies and/or television.

There's nothing wrong with presenting angels as good guys. Yes, the Bible teaches there are ministering angels assigned to help and encourage the saints (See Hebrews 1:14). However, in the Hebrew culture, angels are viewed with great reverence, awe, and fear. In the Bible, angels are described as fierce warriors, messengers of God, and protectors of the throne.

They had helped Jesus before, so why not now? After His temptation in the wilderness, for instance, we are told by Matthew that *"angels came and ministered to Him"* (Matthew 4:11). And, when Jesus was sweating it out in the garden over God's cup of wrath, Luke tells us that *"an angel appeared to Him from heaven, strengthening Him"* (Luke 22:43).

Consider for a moment what Jesus had at His disposal. The Bible tells us that when God removed man from the Garden of Eden, a single angel, a cherubim with a flaming sword, was all that was needed to protect this paradise (Genesis 3:24). It took only one angel of the Lord to kill all the firstborn of Egypt during the night of the Passover (Exodus 12). God sent an angel before the Israelites to drive out the Canaanites, Amorites, Hittites, Perizzites, Hivites, and Jebusites from the Promised Land (Exodus 33:2). An army of angels surrounded Elisha and his servant and struck blind the entire army of the Syrians (2 Kings 6). In one night, the angel of the Lord put to death 185,000 men in the Assyrian army camped before Jerusalem (Isaiah 37:36). The angel of the Lord protected the three friends of Daniel who were thrown in the fiery furnace (Daniel 3:28). God's angels shut the mouths of the lions so Daniel was not harmed by them when he was cast into the lion's den (Daniel 6:22).

If Jesus had called on them, thousands of angels would have made a mockery of human swords and clubs. Against them, all human efforts to capture the King of Glory would come to nothing. He had some rather fierce and powerful creatures at His command:

1. Cherubim

These are angelic beings involved in the worship and praise of God, not some cute chubby figure depicted on Valentine's Day. The cherubim are first mentioned in the Bible in Genesis 3:24: *"So He drove out the man; and he placed cherubim at the east of the garden of Eden, and a flaming sword which turned every way, to guard the way to the tree of life."*

Prior to his rebellion, Satan was a cherub (Ezekiel 28:12-15). The tabernacle and temple along with their articles contained many representations of cherubim (Exodus 25:17-22; 26:1,31; 36:8; 1 Kings 6:23-35; 7:29-36; 8:6-7; 1 Chronicles 28:18; 2 Chronicles 3:7-14; 2 Chronicles 3:10-13; 5:7-8; Hebrews 9:5).

Chapters 1 and 10 of the book of Ezekiel describe the *"four living creatures"* (Ezekiel 1:5) as the same beings as the cherubim (Ezekiel 10). Each had four faces—that of a man, a lion, an ox, and an eagle (Ezekiel 1:10; 10:14)—and each had four wings. In their appearance, the cherubim *"had the likeness of a man"* (Ezekiel 1:5). These cherubim used two of their wings for flying and the other two for covering their bodies (Ezekiel 1:6,11,23). Under their wings the cherubim appeared to have the form, or likeness, of a man's hand (Ezekiel 1:8; 10:7-8,21).

The imagery of Revelation 4:6-9 also seems to be describing cherubs, which served the purpose of magnifying the holiness and power of God. This is one of their main responsibilities throughout the Bible. In addition to singing the Lord's praises, they also were a visible reminder of the majesty and glory of God and His abiding presence with His people.

Cherubs have two responsibilities: first, to guard the presence of God. In the temple the veil was hung before the holy of holies with 30-foot-high cherubs facing each other. Second, in the tabernacle of Moses they are facing each other on top of the Ark of the Covenant pointing to God. The message of the cherubim is, "Get back or die!" When you mentioned cherub to a Hebrew, he would always equate it with the holy presence of God.

2. Seraphim

These "fiery, burning ones," are angelic beings associated with the prophet Isaiah's vision of God in the temple when he was called to his prophetic ministry (Isaiah 6:1-7).

Isaiah 6:2-4 records, *"Above it stood seraphim; each one had six wings: with two he covered his face, with two he covered his feet, and with two he flew. And one cried to another and said: 'Holy, holy, holy is the Lord of hosts; the whole earth is full of His glory!' And the posts of the door were shaken by the voice of him who cried out, and the house was filled with smoke."*

Seraphs are angels that worship God continually. Isaiah chapter 6 is the only place in the Bible that specifically mentions the seraphim. The seraphim flew around the throne on which God was seated, singing His praises as they called special attention to His glory and majesty. These beings apparently also served as agents of purification for Isaiah as he began his prophetic ministry.

One placed a hot coal against Isaiah's lips with the words, *"Your iniquity is taken away, and your sin purged"* (Isaiah 6:7).

The angels were not called.

Since we are told that one single angel was able to wipe out 185,000 men in one night (Isaiah 37:36), it would mean the combined power and strength in one legion of 6,000 angels would be enough to destroy 1 billion, 110 million men, and that's just one legion! The combined strength of 72,000 angels would be enough to wipe out and annihilate at least 13 billion, 320 million—double the number of people now living on planet earth!

There is no doubt in my mind that looking over the ramparts of heaven before the impending crucifixion was a rapid reaction force of angels just waiting for one word to spring into action. Instead of issuing the attack order, Jesus willingly submits to His arrest. He was ready to go through the necessary steps in order not just to cover sin, but to remove sin's stain once and for all. His yoke is teaching a better way.

For thousands of years, God's presence remained behind the veil guarded by the cherub, and for centuries the only way man could approach God was through a blood sacrifice. It did not remove sin, it was only a temporary covering. It would take the ultimate sacrifice of God's son, "the Lamb slain from the foundation of the earth," to remove the guilt, shame, and condemnation of sin.

So, that night in the Garden of Gethsemane, the only thing in the mind of the Hebrew onlookers was: Man–Cherub–God. Touch God and die! So with the thought of death in mind, it's no wonder when Jesus said He could call on twelve legions of angels, they trembled at the thought. Why? Because they had never before been that close to God!

In essence Jesus was telling them, "You have no idea Who you are about to touch. You're not coming to arrest Jesus of Nazareth, or Jesus the Rabbi, you are about to put your hands on "I AM!"

The major lesson to learn from the garden experience is this: the arm of the flesh can never accomplish what one word from the lips of Jesus can do. Christ did not need His disciples to fight on His behalf, especially Peter with his insignificant sword. His yoke was saying, "You don't need the weapons of your flesh to conquer the enemy, I have the power to deal with any problem you experience. The next time you're tempted to handle the enemy with your limited power, stop long enough to remind yourself that "I AM" can handle any opposition or demonic pressure without your help. My yoke is always a better way!

Event #5: At Calvary: the contrast between death and life (Matthew 27:32-36).

"But when they came to Jesus and found that he was already dead, they did not break his legs. Instead, one of the soldiers pierced Jesus' side with a spear, bringing a sudden flow of blood and water. The man who saw it has given testimony, and his testimony is true. He knows that he tells the truth, and he testifies so that you also may believe" (John 19:33-35 NIV).

First the natural, then the spiritual.

Jesus suffered physical pain; what historians describe as the most horrific death that could be inflicted on a human being.

To better understand what He endured, look at the crucifixion from a physician's perspective. The following is adapted from C. Truman Davis, M.D., in *The Expositor's Bible Commentary.*

> *The cross is placed on the ground and the exhausted man is quickly thrown backwards with his shoulders against the wood. The legionnaire feels for the depression at the front of the wrist. He drives a heavy, square wrought-iron nail through the wrist and deep into the wood. Quickly he moves to the other side and repeats the action, being careful not to pull the arms too tightly, but to allow some flex and movement. The cross is then lifted into place.*
>
> *The left foot is pressed backward against the right foot, and with both feet extended, toes down, a nail is driven through the arch of each, leaving the knees flexed. The victim is now crucified.*
>
> *As he slowly sags down with more weight on the nails in the wrists, excruciating, fiery pain shoots along the*

fingers and up the arms to explode in the brain—the nails in the wrists are putting pressure on the median nerves. As he pushes himself upward to avoid this stretching torment, he places the full weight on the nail through his feet. Again he feels the searing agony of the nail tearing through the nerves between the bones of his feet. As the arms fatigue, cramps sweep through the muscles, knotting them in deep, relentless, throbbing pain.

With these cramps comes the inability to push himself upward to breathe. Air can be drawn into the lungs but not exhaled. He fights to raise himself in order to get even one small breath. Finally carbon dioxide builds up in the lungs and in the blood stream, and the cramps partially subside. Spasmodically he is able to push himself upward to exhale and bring in life-giving oxygen.

Hours of this limitless pain, cycles of twisting, joint-rending cramps, intermittent partial asphyxiation, searing pain as tissue is torn from his lacerated back as he moves up and down against the rough timber. Then another agony begins: a deep, crushing pain deep in the chest as the pericardium slowly fills with serum and begins to compress the heart. It is now almost over—the loss of tissue fluids has reached a critical level—the compressed heart is struggling to pump heavy, thick, sluggish blood into the tissues—the tortured lungs are making a frantic effort to gasp in small gulps of air. He can feel the chill of death creeping through His tissues...Finally he can allow his body to die.

All this the Bible records with the simple words, "And they crucified Him." (Mark 15:24). What wondrous love is this?

In the natural, the Gospel writers recorded the historical facts of the crucifixion of Jesus. While they witnessed the arrest, trial, beating, and crucifixion along with all the details, we have to combine Old Testament prophecies with the written record of the authors of the New Testament to explain the spiritual meaning of His death.

1. Messiah would be falsely accused (Psalm 35:11; Mark 14:57-58).
2. Messiah would be silent before His accusers (Isaiah 53:7; Mark 15:4-5).
3. Messiah would be spat upon and struck (Isaiah 50:6; Matthew 26:67).
4. Messiah would be hated without cause (Psalm 35:19; Psalm 69:4; John 15:24-25).
5. Messiah would be crucified with criminals (Isaiah 53:12; Matthew 27:38; Mark 15:27-28).
6. Messiah would be given vinegar to drink (Psalm 69:21; Matthew 27:34; John 19:28-30).
7. Messiah's hands and feet would be pierced (Psalm 22:16; Zechariah 12:10; John 20:25-27).
8. Messiah would be mocked and ridiculed (Psalm 22:7-8; Luke 23:35).
9. Soldiers would gamble for Messiah's garments (Psalm 22:18; Luke 23:34; Matthew 27:35-36).
10. Messiah's bones would not be broken (Exodus 12:46; Psalm 34:20; John 19:33-36).
11. Messiah would be forsaken by God (Psalm 22:1; Matthew 27:46).
12. Messiah would pray for His enemies (Psalm 109:4; Luke 23:34).
13. Soldiers would pierce Messiah's side (John 19:33-35).

The prophet Zechariah prophesied the "fountain" from which we would be cleansed (Zechariah 13:1). That fountain is referring to the blood and water that flowed from Jesus' side, representing the cleansing of our sins.

Since the piercing of His side, and the flow of water and blood is only recorded by John, I believe there is a higher meaning to this historical fact. Scholars and theologians have voiced their opinions on the water in the blood. Songwriters have written eloquently about it: *"Rock of ages cleft for me, let me hide myself in Thee. Let the water and the blood, from Thy wounded side which flowed, be of sin a double cure, save from wrath and make me pure."*

What is the real message of blood and water that came from the cross? I believe it is the continuation of a theme of prophetic portraits in the Scripture that gives us a revelation about the true spiritual meaning.

When we go back to Genesis, we see the genius of God. When sin entered, and Adam and Eve were banished from the garden of delight, or perfection, God was already making plans for redemption.

As the Bible describes, *"A river watering the garden flowed from Eden; from there it was separated into four headwaters. The name of the first is the Pishon; it winds through the entire land of Havilah, where there is gold. (The gold of that land is good; aromatic resin and onyx are also there.)"* (Genesis 2:10-12 NIV).

A RIVER OF HOPE

Flowing out of the garden was a river that separated into four headwaters. One of the four was Pishon, which means "hope." It is written that Havilah is the land of pure gold; and perfect gold is found in the river Pishon. It is more than interesting that the meaning of the word Havilah is "suffering." What's more, water flowing through perfect gold turns blood red.

Since the river Pishon equals hope, and the land of Havilah equals suffering, when you combine them together you have a river of hope in the land of suffering!

The Talmud (the extra-biblical writings of the rabbis), says when Adam and Eve were kicked out of the garden they spent forty days with their feet in the river Pishon (hope). The message to them and to us is this; after sin came death—and suffering was inevitable. But hope can flow through the land of suffering.

- The river hope is seen in Egypt. The first plague, which was a sign to the Hebrews, and a curse to Egypt was bloody water! The curse of slavery was broken.
- The river of hope is seen at Mount Sinai. Moses ground the golden idol to powder. God turned their idols into a river of hope to redeem them from their suffering. The curse of idolatry was shattered.
- The river of hope is seen in the wedding of Cana. Jesus turned their disappointment into joy by turning water into a blood-red wine. The curse of disappointment was lifted.
- The river of hope is seen in the New Jerusalem. *"...and the city was pure gold, like clear glass"* (Revelation 21:18). *"And he showed me a pure river of water of life, clear as crystal, proceeding from the throne of God and of the Lamb"* (Revelation 22:1). I believe somewhere out from the throne where the river of life flows through the city of gold it gives off the illumination of red blood! There is hope for the future!
- The river of hope flowed from the side of Jesus at Calvary. When water and blood came from His side, it was a message to the world: "If you are living in the land of suffering, there is a river of hope!"

From the very beginning, until this very day, every Hebrew was taught that hope flows through suffering when the river turns to blood. *"There is a fountain filled with blood drawn from Immanuel's veins; and sinners, plunged beneath that flood, lose all their guilty stains."*

The birth of Jesus was a paradigm shift that changed the course of history! When Jesus stepped down out of heaven, taking the form of human flesh, He left the protection of the cherubim, stepped from behind the curtain of glory, and declared, "I will tabernacle (make my dwelling) among men" (See Leviticus 26:11; Revelation 21:3).

Each time God touched man:

- The lame walked.

- The blind saw.
- The deaf heard.
- The dead lived.

Sinful men could come and touch God and be forgiven!

The last full measure of devotion was demonstrated at the cross—and the last full measure of redemption was completed at the empty tomb. Sin no longer had to be "covered" with the blood of animals. Now, in the crimson flow of Calvary, sin has been dealt with once and for all! (Hebrews 9:12).

The yoke of Jesus has made it possible for God and man to come together. The righteousness of God demanded death upon all sin. Yet He withheld judgment. Why? To demonstrate His righteousness:

> *But now apart from the law the righteousness of God has been made known, to which the Law and the Prophets testify. This righteousness is given through faith in Jesus Christ to all who believe. There is no difference between Jew and Gentile, for all have sinned and fall short of the glory of God, and all are justified freely by his grace through the redemption that came by Christ Jesus. God presented Christ as a sacrifice of atonement, through the shedding of his blood—to be received by faith.*
>
> *He did this to demonstrate his righteousness, because in his forbearance he had left the sins committed beforehand unpunished—he did it to demonstrate his righteousness at the present time, so as to be just and the one who justifies those who have faith in Jesus* (Romans 3:21-26 NIV).

You see, God had a problem. How could He fellowship and restore His relationship with fallen man? Something had to be done, so He took action.

When I came to Jesus repenting of my sin, trusting Christ as my Lord and Savior, God declared me righteous, in right standing with Him. To be declared "justified" (just as if I'd never sinned) means I can now have free and total access to the Father.

WE ARE JUSTIFIED

The Purpose of Justification

- To remove the guilt of sin (Romans 3:19-20).
- To restore us to God's favor (2 Corinthians 5:21).

The Possibility of Justification

- It was provided by grace (Romans 3:24).
- It was procured by blood (Romans 5:8-9; 1 Peter; 1:17-21).
- It was possessed by faith (Romans 3:27-29; 4:9-25).

The Preciousness of Justification

- It brings peace with God (Romans 5:1-2).
- It brings power to live right (Romans 8:1).
- It brings preservation from wrath (Romans 5:9-11).
- It brings the promise of glorification (Romans 8:28-30).

I have been declared not guilty and there is no record of my sin. The slate has been wiped clean because I have been purchased from the slave market of sin and adopted by a King! I now have royal blood flowing through my veins. Yes, I am a King's kid!

"*He did not enter by means of the blood of goats and calves; but he entered the Most Holy Place once for all by his own blood, thus obtaining eternal redemption* (Hebrews 9:12 NIV).

Remember, the cherubim protected His glory. Jesus came out from behind them so that we may touch God—and He may touch man. The wrath that we deserved was placed on Jesus, and as a result of His death, burial, and resurrection, the blood was sprinkled on the mercy seat of heaven. He could now take us past the cherubim to the throne of God where we are seated in heavenly places!

The message of Rabbi Jesus (His yoke) is:

- When you become nothing, you become everything!
- In order to be like Jesus, you must die!

• When you die, others will live!

In Christ you are; sons not slaves, saints not sinners, royalty and not paupers! *"Since...you have been raised with Christ, set your hearts on things above, where Christ is, seated at the right hand of God* (Colossians 3:1 NIV).

What took place at Calvary has transformed the lives of millions—in every corner of the world. My heart was touched when I read the story of Fanny Crosby, one of the most beloved hymn writers of all time. The following is adapted from her biography:

> *In her infancy, Fanny Crosby became totally blind. Yet in her affliction she wrote over 8,000 hymns, many of which are still being sung today. Some that you will know include; "Blessed Assurance," "Near the Cross," "To God Be the Glory," Pass Me Not O Gentle Savior, "Rescue the Perishing," and "Sweet Hour of Prayer."*
>
> *Once a preacher sympathetically remarked, "I think it is a great pity that the Master did not give you sight when He showered so many other gifts upon you." She replied quickly, "Do you know that if at birth I had been able to make one petition, it would have been that I should be born blind?" "Why?" asked the surprised minister. "Because when I get to heaven, the first face that shall ever gladden my sight will be that of my Savior!"*
>
> *Near the end of the nineteenth century, Fanny was visiting the Lake Chautauqua Institute, in Western New York State. In those days this was a place for Christian fellowship, great preaching, and singing of wonderful hymns. It was here that she met John R. Sweney.*
>
> *After a busy day at the camp meeting, both were taking a rest on the front porch of the grand hotel when John posed an interesting question. "Fanny," he asked, "do you think we'll recognize our friends in heaven?"*
>
> *Initially her response was positive. She then added, "John, that's not what you really want to know. You wonder how an old lady who has been blind all her life*

could even recognize one person, let alone her Lord and Savior. Well I've given it a lot of thought and I don't think I'll have a problem. But if I do, when I get to heaven, I'm going to look around and when I see the one who I think is my Savior, I'm going to walk up to Him and say, 'May I see your hands?' When I see the nail prints in the hands of my Savior, then I'll know I've found my Jesus."

"Oh Fanny," John said, "That would make a great song." "No thank you," she replied. "I'm tired, I'm going to bed." Well the next morning, bright and early, Fanny met John for breakfast and before they went their separate ways, she dictated the words of this great hymn. It has always been one of my favorite hymns because it is about heaven and the hope of each Christian should be to see our Lord, face to face. What a wonderful day that will be!

When my life work is ended, and I cross the swelling tide,
When the bright and glorious morning I shall see
I shall know my Redeemer when I reach the other side,
And His smile will be the first to welcome me.
I shall know Him, I shall know Him
And redeemed by His side, I shall stand.
I shall know Him, I shall know Him,
By the print of the nails in His hand.

Hallelujah What a Savior!

As believers, our responsibility in this present age is to repeat what our Rabbi has taught us. We do not have the right or authority (Semicha) to reinterpret His yoke through the lens of our own personal biases or taste. It is incumbent upon each one of us to obey the clear command of our Rabbi: *"Therefore go and make disciples of all nations, baptizing them in the name of the Father and of the Son and of the Holy Spirit, and teaching them to obey everything I have commanded you (His yoke). And surely I am with you always, to the very end of the age"* (Matthew 28:19-20 NIV).

Jesus is still asking, *"Are you tired? Worn out? Burned out on religion? Come to me. Get away with me and you'll recover your life. I'll show you how to take a real rest. Walk with me and work with me—watch how I do it. Learn the unforced rhythms of grace. I won't lay anything heavy or ill-fitting on you. Keep company with me and you'll learn to live freely and lightly"* (Matthew 11:28-30 MSG).

The yoke of Jesus the Rabbi is a better way of life. I invite you to walk in it today!

Endnotes

Chapter 1

Dallas Willard, Hearing God: Developing a Conversational Relationship with God, http://www.goodreads.com

Rick Warren, How to Hear God Speak, excerpted from a message. Saddleback Resources.

Sandy Warner, Eagle Facts and Parables of Mentoring, http://The QuickenedWord.com

Soren Kierkegaard: *Our Daily Bread,* March 15, 1994, http://www.sermonillustrations.com

Jaroslav Pelikan, *The Vindication of Tradition,* http://www.goodreads.com

Aaron Bartmess, *From The Pastor's Desk,* April 2010, http://edgemontpres.org

Chapter 2

Frank Outlaw: http://thinkexist.com

John F. Kennedy, Inaugural Address, January 20, 1961. Public domain.

Winston Churchill, speaking to the House of Commons, June 4, 1940. Public domain.

Thomas Jefferson, Declaration of Independence 1776. Public domain.

Charles Henrickson: Blog at http://WordPress.com

Chapter 3

Thomas Watson: http://christian-quotes.ochristian.com

Elyah Israel, *The Hebrew Bible is the Mind of God.* http://EzineArticles.com

The Cathode Ray, The Christian Herald. http://www.thechristianherald.info

A Sweet Little Six-Year-Old Girl. http://www.searchquotes.com/search/Onward/

The Judas Tree, The Christian Herald. http://www.thechristianherald.info

Dr. F. E. Marsh: *Knight's Master Book of New Illustrations.* http://www.sermoncentral.com/illustrations

Chapter 4

Mother Teresa. http://www.brainyquote.tumblr.com

What is Christian Holiness? Excerpted from http://MinistryMatters.com/holiness
J. C. Ryle: http://Christian.com.
Professor H. Hanko, http://www.prca.org
Max Lucado, Excerpted from an article on Forgiveness, http://MinistryMatters.com.

Chapter 5

Charles Spurgeon, in *Wycliffe Handbook of Preaching and Preachers,* W. Wiersbe, Victor Books, Wheaton, IL.
J. Stowell, *Fan the Flame,* Moody, 1986, p.13.
Daniel Taylor, *The Myth of Certainty.* http://www.goodreads.com
Patrick Henry, *John Bartlett's Familiar Quotations.* http://thinkexist.com/quotes/
Peter Marshall. http://www.liberty-virtue-independence.blogspot.com/2011/08/prayers-of-reverend-peter-marshall.html
S. Louis Johnson, *The Paralysis of Legalism.* Excerpted from an article in Theological Quarterly.
Wendell Phillips: http://www.thinkexist.com
Eugene H. Peterson, *Traveling Light.* http://www.gci.org/book/Peterson

Chapter 6

Henri J. M. Nouwen. http://dailychristianquote.com
"Coronary and Ulcer Club," *Bits & Pieces,* January 7, 1993, http://www.sermonillustrations.com/a-z/b/burnout.htm
The Crash of Avianca Flight 52. http://www.nytimes.com/1990/02/05/
George MacDonald:http://thinkexist.com/quotes
Daniel R. Vess, Excerpted from a sermon. http://www.forumterrace.com

Chapter 7

A. W. Tozer. http://www.christian-quotes.ochristian.com/A.W.-Tozer-Quotes
A. W. Pink. http://www.preach-the-gospel.com/A-W-Pink-Quotes
Frederick W. Robertson. http://www.fwrobertson.com

Chapter 8

Mark Twain. http;//www.brainyquote.com
Brian Knowles, Excerpted from *Hebraism and Hellenism* by William

Barrett. http://www.godward.org
Don Ratzlaff, *Ernest Gordon's Miracle on the River Kwai.* http://www.sermonillustrations.com
Scott L. Harris, Excerpted from a sermon. http://www.gracebibleny.org

Chapter 9

Jerry Bridges: http://www.goodreads.com
Dave Scriven, *Word Traveler.* http://www.open.salon.com/blog
Michell Dillon, *Story of Whitney Houston.* http://www.illustrationexchange.com
Fred Wright, *The Barren Fig Tree.* http://www.marshill.com
Ian Sweeny. http://www.saltforsermons.org.
E. M. Bounds: http://www.biblebelievers.com

Chapter 10

C.T. Studd: http://www.wholesomewords.org
Dr. David Miller, http://www.cbn.com/SpiritualLife/A Physician's View of the Crucifixion
C. Truman Davis, M.D, adapted from *The Expositor's Bible Commentary,* Vol. 8
Fanny Crosby. Adapted from biography. http://www.wholesomewords.org/biography

Bibliography

Benson, Carmen: *Jesus and Israel*, Charisma Books, Watchung, NJ.

Buford, Bob: *Half Time*, Zondervan Publishing House, Grand Rapids, MI.

Chambers, Oswald: *My Utmost for His Highest*, Barbour and Company, Inc. Westwood, NJ.

Crockett, Kent: *The 911 Handbook*, Hendrickson Publishers, Peabody, MA.

Dorsett, Lyle: *A Passion for Souls—The Life of Dwight L. Moody*, Zondervan Publishing House, Grand Rapids, MI.

Edersheim, Alfred: *The Temple—Its Ministry and Services*, Hendrickson Publishers, Peabody, MA.

______: *The Life and Times of Jesus the Messiah*, Hendrickson Publishers, Peabody, MA

Kolatch, Alfred J.: *The Jewish Book of Why*, Jonathan David Publishers, Middle Village, NY.

Lewis, C.S.: *The Four Loves*, HarperCollins Publishers, New York, NY.

Maimonides, Moses: *Mishneh Torah, Hilchot Talmud Torah 1:8*, Maimonides and Moznaim Publishers.

Meyer, Joyce: *How to Hear from God*, Warner Faith, Time Warner Book Group, New York, NY.

Munroe, Myles: *Releasing Your Potential*, Destiny Image Publishing, Shippensburg, PA.

______: *The Purpose and Power of Praise and Worship*, Destiny Image Publishing, Shippensburg, PA.

Phillips, John: *Exploring the World of the Jew*, Moody Publishers, Chicago, IL.

Renner, Rick: *Sparkling Gems from the Greek*, Teach All Nations Publishing, Tulsa, OK.

Spangler, Ann and Tverberg, Lois: *Sitting at the Feet of Rabbi Jesus*, Zondervan Publishing House, Grand Rapids, MI.

Wiersbe, Warren: *Encouragement for Difficult Days*, Victor Books, Wheaton IL.

______: *Be Free*, Victor Books, Wheaton, IL.

Young, Brad: *Jesus the Jewish Theologian*, Gospel Research Foundation, Inc., Tulsa, OK.

NOTES

For Additional Resources
or to Schedule the Author for
Speaking Engagements,
Contact:

Dwain Miller
Cross Life Church
1010 Combs Street
El Dorado, Arkansas, 71730

Phone: 870-863-7626

Email: dwain@crosslifechurch.net

Internet: www.dwainmiller.com
www.crosslifechurch.net